Careers in Focus

Agriculture

Andrew Morkes, *Managing Editor-Career Publications*
Carol Yehling, *Senior Editor*
Anne Paterson, *Editor*
Nora Walsh, *Editorial Assistant*
Paula Garner, *Additional Editorial Assistance*

Library of Congress Cataloging-in-Publication Data

Careers in focus. Agriculture.
p. cm.
ISBN 0-89434-328-9 (hardcover : alk. paper)
1. Agriculture--Vocational guidance--United States--Juvenile literature. [1. Agriculture--Vocational guidance. 2. Vocational guidance.] I. Title: Agriculture. II. J.G. Ferguson Publishing Company.

S494.5.A4 C27 2001
630'.2'03--dc21

00-012767

Printed in the United States of America

Cover photo courtesy Roy Morsch/Stockmarket

Published and distributed by
Ferguson Publishing Company
200 West Jackson Boulevard, 7th Floor
Chicago, Illinois 60606
800-306-9941
www.fergpubco.com

Y-2

Table of Contents

Introduction

The American agricultural industry is vast and diverse. It is made up of *Farmers* who cultivate the land, raise livestock, and grow plants; the workers who purchase, process, distribute, and transport farm products and farm supplies, such as *Canning and Preserving Industry Workers* and *Dairy Products Manufacturing Workers*; and the workers who supply services to the farmer and the consumer, including *Farm Equipment Mechanics*, *Food Technologists*, and *Soil Conservationists and Technicians*. This whole complex network of activities is often called agribusiness.

According to the United States Department of Agriculture, agribusiness employs 15 percent of the U.S. labor force. Despite recent decline, farmers still feed the nation and the world, and innovative uses for commodities are opening new markets. Advances in science and technology have made agricultural production much more efficient, but also more complex, calling upon the skills of *Agribusiness Technicians, Agricultural Consultants*, and other agricultural professionals.

The base for all agricultural work is the farm. The average farm is run by a farm operator or a farm manager, who in most cases has attended college and earned an agricultural degree. Farms usually employ both permanent and seasonal workers. Part-time employees work during the harvest and planting seasons, and permanent employees are responsible for the day-to-day operations of the farm throughout the year.

Single crop farms are commonplace. On these farms, the cash crop (the crop that is grown for sale) is the only thing produced. Wheat and corn single crop farms are widespread throughout the Midwest. Specialized livestock production is mainly centered on cattle and poultry operations in the United States. Sheep, goat, turkey, and aquaculture (fish) farms are examples of single livestock operations.

Diversified farms produce several different crops or animals, or a mixture of both, for sale. The old-style family farm was often a diversified farm. These farms are less common now, partly because of the simplicity of specialized production, but mainly because the profit margin is often higher with single-crop production. Land is normally well suited to only a few types of plants or animals, which makes diversification difficult. However, the diversified farm is less dependent on the success of a single item. Drought, disease, and other natural disasters may take less of a toll on the farm that produces many different products.

Farmers often depend on off-the-farm industries to provide seed, fertilizer, and machinery. After the crops are harvested or cattle are bred, output industries process and market the farm products. Storage, shipping, processing, packaging, and canning are just some of the industries that assist the farmer in the sale of goods. For example, *Grain Merchants* assist farmers by acting as the liaison between the farmer and the consumer. After they purchase the grain directly from the farmer, they inspect it for quality, then process, store, and market the grain out to the public.

To ensure sales of their produce, farmers can arrange to sell their crops before producing them. This process, known as "hedging," has benefits for both the farmer and the buyer. A contract is drawn up to ship produce to the buyer upon harvesting. The farmer must agree to a price at the time of the contract. If the weather is favorable and crops are good, farmers face more competition. A contract helps farmers get higher prices than if they had to bid against other farmers selling the same crop. On the other hand, if crop production is low, then buyers benefit from a contract agreement, obtaining the crop at a cheaper rate than the going market price. This process of contractual buying and selling of crops is handled by *Commodities Brokers*, who are the agents who carry out the buying and selling of commodities, such as farm crops.

The off-the-farm portion of the agricultural industry, in addition to offering goods and services, also provides many diverse and interesting careers. Of the approximately 21 million people working in various areas of agriculture, only about 2 million work on farms, whereas about 19 million work in agricultural jobs off the farm.

In 1862, the U.S. Congress gave each state a land grant that consisted of 30,000 acres of land for each senator and representative in Congress. The state was to sell the land and use the proceeds to build a college that would specialize in education for agriculture and engineering. Some states created new universities, and some funded colleges and universities that were already established. The University of Illinois and the University of California are two well-known land-grant universities. State universities with agricultural schools are usually affiliated with research centers called agricultural experiment stations.

Experiment stations conduct research on farming techniques to develop the most effective methods of farming for each region. Workers such as *Agricultural Scientists, Farm Crop Production Technicians*, and *Soil Scientists* work with soils, crops, feed rations, animals, plant variations, and genetic strains to devise the best farming method for the climate and the zone in which they work. Some states have several stations working in different areas to account for regional differences.

Some careers in agriculture are experiencing a period of decline. Workers who are employed by an individual farm or farm-related industry (such as dairy products manufacturing workers) may find less opportunities because technology is replacing workers with machinery—eliminating the need for many positions. On the other hand, those working in scientific and research positions with advanced degrees are likely to encounter more diverse career opportunities. Agricultural scientists, agribusiness technicians, and other specialists are involved in high-tech methods of conservation, planting, tilling, and treating farm crops, and as a result, are more in demand. To keep up with changing agricultural methods, farmers will need extensive education and training to keep current with new farming methods and equipment as well as computer-aided operations. In the past, land was treated more generally—as if every acre had the same needs. More recently, scientists and farmers have discovered that soil and plants are highly distinctive, and better treated as specifically as possible. "Precision farming" using computers, satellites, and sensors now treat each type of soil and plant for its own needs. Farm equipment has become more technical. Tractors are now able to be programmed in order to administer the precise amount of fertilizer and herbicide needed by a given soil or plant. Farmers will be able to treat their land with more effective fertilizers and pesticides, and their genetically engineered crops will be more resistant to drought and disease.

In many agriculture-based states, adding value to locally grown produce is a significant wealth and job creator. Discovering new uses for crops will provide many jobs for those involved in processing and marketing. For example, corn is used for ethanol, sweeteners, feed products, corn oil, and lactic acid. Studies are underway that will expand corn's uses to include adhesives, paper and packaging, nonprescription medical products, and even plastic.

Each article in this book discusses a particular agriculture industry occupation in detail. Many of the articles in *Careers in Focus: Agriculture* appear in Ferguson's *Encyclopedia of Careers and Vocational Guidance*—but have been updated and revised with the latest information from the U.S. Department of Labor and other sources. Additionally, a new article, *Beekeepers*, has been specifically written for this book. The **Overview** section is a brief introductory description of the duties and responsibilities of someone in the career. Oftentimes, a career may have a variety of job titles. When this is the case, alternative career titles are presented in this section. The **History** section describes the history of the particular job as it relates to the overall development of its industry or field. The **Job** describes the primary and secondary duties of the job. **Requirements** discusses high school and postsecondary education and training requirements, any certification or licensing necessary, and any other personal requirements for success in the job. **Exploring** offers suggestions on how to gain some experience in or knowledge of the particular job before making a firm educational and financial commitment. The focus is on what can be done while still in high school (or in the early years of college) to gain a better understanding of the job. The **Employers** section gives an overview of typical places of employment for the job. **Starting Out** discusses the best ways to land that first job, be it through the college placement office, newspaper ads, or personal contact. The **Advancement** section describes what kind of career path to expect from the job and how to get there. **Earnings** lists salary ranges and describes the typical fringe benefits. The **Work Environment** section describes the typical surroundings and conditions of employment—whether indoors or outdoors, noisy or quiet, social or independent, and so on. Also discussed are typical hours worked, any seasonal fluctuations, and the stresses and strains of the job. The **Outlook** section summarizes the job in terms of the general economy and industry projections. For the most part, Outlook information is obtained from the Bureau of Labor Statistics and is supplemented by information taken from professional associations. Job growth terms follow those used in the *Occupational Outlook Handbook*: Growth described as "much faster than the average" means an increase of 36 percent or more. Growth described as "faster than the average" means an increase of 21 to 35 percent. Growth described as "about as fast as the average" means an increase of 10 to 20 percent. Growth described as "little change or more slowly than the average" means an increase of 0 to 9 percent. "Decline" means a decrease of 1 percent or more. Each article ends with **For More Information**, which lists organizations that can provide career information on training, education, internships, scholarships, and job placement.

Agribusiness Technicians

School Subjects
Agriculture
Business

Personal Skills
Leadership/management
Technical/scientific

Work Environment
Indoors and outdoors
Primarily multiple locations

Minimum Education Level
Associate's degree

Salary Range
$18,000 to $23,000 to $40,000

Certification or Licensing
None available

Outlook
About as fast as the average

Overview

Agribusiness technicians combine their agriculture and business backgrounds to manage or offer management consulting services to farms and agricultural businesses. Agribusiness technicians, also called *agricultural business technicians*, generally work as liaisons between farms and agricultural businesses, representing either the farm or the business.

History

The marketing of agricultural products first concerned farmers in the early 20th century. Cooperative organizations were formed in the 1920s, allowing farmers to control the marketing of their commodities, but farmers still struggled to make profits. It was about this time that the field of agricultural economics evolved; the International Association of Agricultural Economics was established in 1929.

The Dust Bowl of the 1930s complicated farm economics further, leading to New Deal legislation. Under the New Deal, which enacted the first effective farm legislation in the United States, the secretary of agriculture could control crop production. In the following years, agriculture expanded as a result of scientific advances and better methods of planting and harvesting. By the 1960s, marketing had become much more complicated for farmers, leading to the development of agribusiness as a major career field. Today, agribusiness is much larger than the farming industry; two-thirds of each dollar spent on food goes toward processing, packaging, marketing, and retailing, with only one-third going to the farm.

The Job

Agribusiness is as diverse a field as agriculture, and involves professionals in economics, sales, marketing, commodities, science, and other areas. Technicians assist these professionals. They may work for a farm or for a business or organization that assists farmers. They may spend their workdays out in the field or behind a desk or a combination of these two. Their work may focus on such areas as grain, livestock, or dairy farm production.

Some agribusiness technicians choose to go into business management, working as part of a personnel-management office for a large corporate farm or dairy. In such a position, the technician manages staff, coordinates work plans with farm managers, and oversees the entire salary structure for farm or other production workers. Other agribusiness technicians work as *purchasing agents*, supervising all the buying for large commercial farms. Another option for the agribusiness technician is to work as a *farm sales representative*, finding the best markets for the produce of farms on a local, state, or national level. In this capacity, the technician travels a great deal and works closely with records technicians and other personnel of the farm or farms he or she represents.

Some agribusiness technicians assist farmers with record keeping. The records that farmers and other agricultural business people must keep are becoming more detailed and varied every year. Agribusiness technicians may set up complete record-keeping systems. They analyze records and help farmers make management decisions based on the accumulated facts. Computerized record keeping is common now, so there is a tremendous need for *agricultural records technicians* who can create tailor-made programs to help farmers get maximum benefit from their output. Furthermore, they analyze the output and make practical applications of the information.

In some positions, such as *agricultural quality control technician*, the technician works directly with farmers but is employed by another company. *Dairy production field-contact technicians*, for example, serve as contact people between dairy companies and the farms which produce the milk. They negotiate long- or short-term contracts to purchase milk and milk products according to agreed specifications; meet with farmers to test milk for butterfat content, sediment, and bacteria; and discuss ways to solve milk-production problems and improve production. They suggest methods of feeding, housing, and milking to improve production or comply with sanitary regulations. They set up truck routes to haul milk to the dairy; solicit membership in cooperative associations; or even sell items such as dairy-farm equipment, chemicals, and feed to the farmers they contact.

Poultry field-service technicians inspect farms to insure compliance with agreements involving facilities, equipment, sanitation, and efficiency. They advise farmers on how to improve the quality of their products. Technicians may examine chickens for evidence of disease and growth rate to determine the effectiveness of medication and feeding programs. They also recommend changes in equipment or procedures to improve production. They may recommend laboratory testing of feeds, diseased chickens, and diet supplements. In these cases, they often gather samples and take them to a laboratory for analysis. They report their findings on farm conditions, laboratory tests, their own recommendations, and farmers' reactions to the company or association employing them.

Agribusiness technicians may also work for credit institutions which solicit the business of farmers, make appraisals of real estate and personal property, organize and present loan requests, close loans, and service those loans with periodic reviews of the borrower's management performance and financial status. They might also work as *farm representatives* for banks, cooperatives, or federal lending institutions. In this capacity they sell their organizations' services to farmers or agricultural business people, make appraisals, and do the paperwork involved with lending money.

Requirements

High School

In high school, you should take social studies, laboratory science (biology, chemistry, or physics), mathematics, and—if possible—agriculture and business classes. English and composition will be particularly helpful, since oral and written communications are central to the work of the agribusiness technician. Also, take computer classes so that you are familiar with using this technology. Computers are often used in record keeping and production planning.

Postsecondary Training

After completing high school, it is necessary to train in a two-year agricultural or technical college. Many colleges offer associate's degrees in agribusiness or agricultural management. The programs concentrate on basic economic theory; training in management analysis and practical problem-solving; and intensive communications training, such as public speaking and report writing.

Typical first-year courses in an agricultural or technical college include English, biology, health and physical education, introductory animal husbandry, principles of accounting, agricultural economics, microbiology, botany, introductory data processing, soil science, and principles of business.

Typical second-year courses include marketing agricultural commodities, farm management, social science, agricultural finance, agricultural marketing institutions, forage and seed crops, personnel management, and agricultural records and taxation.

Other Requirements

You must be able to work well with other people, which includes being able to delegate responsibility and establish friendly relations with farmers, laborers, and company managers. You must be able to analyze management problems and make sound decisions based on your analysis. And you must have excellent oral and written communications skills: technicians are expected to present written and oral reports, offer comments and advice clearly, and, when necessary, train other workers for a particular job.

Exploring

You should seek summer or part-time employment in your desired specialty—for example, a clerical job in a farm insurance agency or as a laborer in a feed and grain company. Because many technical colleges offer evening courses, it may be possible to obtain permission during your senior year to audit a course or even to take it for future college credit. Work experience on a farm will give you insight into the business concerns of farmers, as will industry periodicals such as *Farm Journal* and *Grain Journal*. Join your high school's chapter of the National FFA Organization (formerly Future Farmers of America) or a local 4-H group, where you may have the opportunity to work on farm-management projects.

Employers

Many different agriculture-based businesses hire graduates of agribusiness programs. Employers include large commercial farms, grain elevators, credit unions, farm equipment dealerships, farm supply stores, fertilizer and processing plants, agricultural chemical companies, and local, state, and federal government agencies.

Starting Out

Your agribusiness program will likely require a semester or more of employment experience, and will assist you in finding an internship or part-time job with agribusiness professionals. Many students are able to turn their internships into full-time work or make connections which lead to other job opportunities. Most agribusiness technician jobs are considered entry-level, or management trainee, positions, and don't require a great deal of previous experience. These jobs are often advertised in the classifieds or posted with career placement centers at community colleges.

Advancement

The ultimate aim of many technicians is to own a business. Technicians can start their own companies in any agricultural business area or act as *freelance agents* under contract to perform specific services for several firms. For example, an experienced agribusiness technician may purchase a computer and data-processing equipment, set up the necessary record-keeping programs, and act as a consulting firm for a host of farms and agricultural businesses.

There are many other positions an agribusiness technician may hold. *Farm managers* oversee all operations of a farm and work closely with owners and other management, customers, and all farm departments on larger farms. *Regional farm credit managers* supervise several of a bank's farm representatives. They may suggest training programs for farm representatives, recommend changes in lending procedures, and conduct personal audits of randomly selected farm accounts. *Sales managers* act as liaisons between company sales representatives and individual dealers, distributors, or farmers.

Earnings

A 1998 salary survey conducted by AGRICAREERS, Inc., found that assistant managers for beef, swine, and crop farms had average salaries of between $21,700 and $26,000 a year. On the low end of the scale, assistant managers averaged $18,000 a year; on the high end, $40,000. A 1997 *Meat and Poultry Magazine* survey found the median base salary for salespeople/sales representatives in the industry to be $36,000 a year.

Fringe benefits vary widely, depending upon the employer. Some amount to as much as one-third of the base salary. More and more employers are providing such benefits as pension plans, paid vacations, insurance, and tuition reimbursement.

Work Environment

Because the field is so large, working environments may be anywhere from a corporate office to a cornfield. Those who work in sales are likely to travel a good deal, with a few nights spent on the road or even a few weeks spent out of the country. Technicians at banks or data-processing services usually work in clean, pleasant surroundings. The technician who goes into farm management or who owns a farm is likely to work outdoors in all kinds of weather.

Agribusiness technicians are often confronted with problems requiring careful thought and decision. They must be able to remain calm when things get hectic, to make sound decisions, and then to stand by their decisions in the face of possible disagreement. It is a profession that requires initiative, self-reliance, and the ability to accept responsibilities which may bring blame at times of failure as well as substantial rewards for successful performance. For those technicians who possess the qualities of leadership and a strong interest in the agricultural business, it can be a challenging, exciting, and highly satisfying profession.

Outlook

According to the U.S. Department of Labor, agribusiness provides employment to about 21 percent of the country's labor force. Despite the fluctuations in the agricultural industry, agribusiness professionals and technicians will continue to be in great demand in the marketing and production of food and other agricultural products.

Agribusiness technicians may find more opportunities to work abroad. Agribusiness plays a large part in global trade issues, and in the government's efforts to support farms and agricultural reforms in other countries, such as the partnership between the United States Department of Agriculture and the Russian Ministry of Agriculture and Food. Agribusiness construction is a subfield that is developing as a result of these reforms; technicians will be needed to assist in the planning and construction of farm-to-market roads in other countries, irrigation channels, bridges, grain silos, and other improvements.

For More Information

To learn about the roles economists play in agriculture, visit the AAEA Web site.

American Agricultural Economics Association (AAEA)
415 South Duff Avenue, Suite C
Ames, IA 50010
Tel: 515-233-3202
Web: http://www.aaea.org

For more information on education and opportunities in the agricultural field, contact:

4-H
Stop 2225
1400 Independence Avenue, SW
Washington, DC 20250-2225
Tel: 202-720-2908
Web: http://www.4h-usa.org

National FFA Organization
6060 FFA Drive
PO Box 68960
Indianapolis, IN 46268
Tel: 317-802-6060
Web: http://www.ffa.org

Agricultural Consultants

School Subjects
Agriculture
Business

Personal Skills
Helping/teaching
Leadership/management

Work Environment
Indoors and outdoors
Primarily multiple locations

Minimum Education Level
Bachelor's degree

Salary Range
$21,370 to $32,380 to $65,983+

Certification or Licensing
None available

Outlook
Decline

Overview

Agricultural consultants, sometimes known as *agricultural extension service workers*, live in rural communities and act as resources for farmers on a range of topics from agricultural technology to the issues facing the modern rural family. They are employed by either the U.S. Department of Agriculture (USDA), various state departments of agriculture, or state agricultural colleges. Agricultural consultants advise farmers on improved methods of agriculture and agricultural work such as farm management, crop rotation, soil conservation, livestock breeding and feeding, use of new machinery, and marketing. They assist individuals wishing to start their own farms, provide the most current agricultural advancements to the community, and speak to the community or local government groups on agricultural issues. They also supervise the work of family and community educators and young people's clubs such as 4-H.

History

In the late 18th century, President George Washington decided to establish an educational agency of the federal government dedicated to assisting the nation's farmers. Washington's proposal eventually developed into what is now known as the Department of Agriculture.

In 1862, President Abraham Lincoln promoted the Morrill Act which established land grant colleges. Under this act, each state was given thirty thousand acres of land for each senator and representative in Congress. The state was to sell the land and use the proceeds to build colleges that would specialize in education for agriculture and engineering.

Once established, the state agricultural colleges were faced with the task of compiling enough data to develop an agricultural curriculum which would be of use to the American farmer. Under the Hatch Act of 1887, experimental stations were created. These agricultural laboratory settings were devoted to gathering information regarding soils, crops, livestock, fruits, and machinery. They became sources of information for both agricultural colleges and farmers.

Land-grant colleges became important resources for agricultural data and education. However, it soon became clear that it would be more effective to send people into the field who were familiar with the farmers' work and who were educated in the agricultural sciences than to expect farmers to leave their work or come from remote areas to attend college classes. Thus the role of the agricultural consultant came into being.

The agricultural extension service was developed and placed in operation in 1914 on a federal basis by the passage of the Smith-Lever Act. The service was opened to any state that wished to join the educational project on a cooperative basis, and most states accepted the opportunity. Because of this, every state agricultural college in the nation today has an extension service as one of its major departmental classifications.

In 1994, the U.S. Department of Agriculture Reorganization Act created the Cooperative State Research, Education and Extension Service (CSREES). CSREES expands the research and higher education functions of the former cooperative State Research Service and the education and outreach functions of the former Extension Service.

The Job

Agricultural consultants teach agricultural subjects at places other than college campuses. The aim of these educational programs is to teach agricultural workers to analyze and solve agricultural problems. They cover such topics as soil and crop improvement, livestock, farm machinery, fertilizers, new methods of planting, and any other subject that may be of assistance to the farmer. Classroom settings are avoided. Rather, the consultants work on-site, possibly while the farmer is engaged in planting or harvesting, or in small evening meetings of five or six farmers. Occasionally, classes are offered in more formal settings during which the consultant speaks before larger groups and makes presentations.

County agricultural agents work closely with federal agricultural agents in gathering information to be presented to the farmers. Information on agronomy (the theory and practice of soil management and crop production), livestock, marketing, agricultural and home economics, horticulture, and entomology (the study of insects) may come either from the state agricultural college or from the CSREES. The county agricultural worker's job is to review the new information, decide what is most pertinent to local operations, and then present it as effectively as possible to the farmers in that particular area. The county or federal extension service agent's work is primarily educational in nature and is aimed at increasing the efficiency of agricultural production and marketing and the development of new and different markets for agricultural products.

County agricultural agents also work closely with *family and community educators*, or *FCE agents*, who assist and instruct families on ways to improve their home life. This work ranges from offering advice and suggestions on preserving fruits and vegetables to improving health care and nutrition, assisting in balancing family budgets, and handling family stress. The FCE agent is responsible for keeping current in every area relating to the rural home and for sharing this information with families in a particular county or group of counties.

4-H Club agents organize and direct the educational projects and activities of the 4-H Club. 4-H educational programs focus on building lifelong learning skills that develop youth potential. An extensive set of programs is designed to engage youth in healthy learning experiences, increasing self-esteem, and problem-solving skills. Programs address stress-management, self-protection, parent-teen communication, personal development, careers, and global understanding. Youth are encouraged to explore science, technology, and citizenship. 4-H Club agents analyze the needs of individuals and the community, develop teaching materials, train volunteers, and organize exhibits at state and county fairs. They also introduce children and adolescents to techniques in raising animals and plants, including breeding, husbandry, and nutrition.

Due to the proliferating advancements in electronic communications technology, there are interesting opportunities for careers in communications with the USDA Extension Service. There is a degree of specialization involved, especially at the federal level. Federal agricultural consultants often become program leaders who are responsible for developing and maintaining relationships with various land-grant colleges, universities, government agencies, and private agencies involved in agriculture. In some cases, they also become *educational research and training specialists* responsible for developing research programs in all phases of consulting work. The results of these programs are shared with the various state agencies.

Subject matter specialists develop programs through which new information can be presented to the farmers effectively. *Educational media specialists* condense information and distribute it as it becomes available to the states for use in their local extension programs. These consultants may be designated *extension service specialists*. An extension service worker who is in charge of programs for a group of counties is a *district extension service agent*.

Requirements

High School

You should follow your high school's college preparatory program and take courses in English, government, foreign language, and history. Also, be sure to take courses in mathematics and the sciences, particularly biology and physics. Computer courses will also be beneficial. Take any economics courses available, along with accounting and business classes, as agricultural consultants are actively involved in farm management.

Postsecondary Training

To do this work, you'll need a bachelor's degree with a major in agriculture or economics. If you hope to join the on-campus staff at the state agricultural college, you'll need at least a master's degree. College courses usually required for this work include English, history, chemistry, biology, economics, education, sociology, and speech, as well as animal science, crop production, horticulture, soils, and farm management. A number of colleges have developed regular agricultural extension curriculums to be followed by those hoping to enter the field.

After finishing college, county agents are kept up-to-date on the latest programs, policies, and teaching techniques through in-service training programs run by the state agricultural college and the Department of Agriculture.

Other Requirements

You'll need a background of practical farming experience and a thorough knowledge of the types of problems confronting farmers, members of rural communities, and their families. Farmers naturally feel more comfortable seeking advice from people whom they feel have a complete understanding of their work.

You must be a good teacher and should enjoy working with people. You must also be assertive, yet diplomatic, and have a particular affinity for farmers and their problems. In addition, you will be expected to organize group projects, meetings, and broad educational programs that both adults and young people involved in agriculture will find stimulating and useful. You'll need the professional interest and enthusiasm that will enable you to keep up with the huge amount of new agricultural information constantly being released. You must be willing to learn and use the latest teaching techniques to disseminate current agricultural practices and knowledge to local residents.

Exploring

To get a sense of the job, you can read the pamphlets and occupational information brochures published by the USDA about this field, and you can request meetings with your local agricultural agent. Any of the state agricultural colleges will send materials or release the name of the local agent for interested students.

Another way to prepare for work in this field is to join groups such as 4-H, National FFA Organization (formerly Future Farmers of America), Future Homemakers of America, and the Boy or Girl Scouts. You may also volunteer to work at an extension office. It may be possible to visit with farmers or others engaged in agriculture to hear their impressions of the work carried on by the agricultural consultants in your particular county.

Employers

Federal agricultural consultants are employed by the USDA to assist county extension officers and supervisors in planning, developing, and coordinating national, regional, and state extension programs. They're headquartered in Washington, D.C. County agricultural agents may be employed jointly by the Department of Agriculture and the agricultural college in each state.

County agents may also specialize, especially in those counties employing more than two or three agents. Many counties with diverse agricultural businesses and farms will often have five or more agents. A single county may employ specialists in fruit and grain production, dairy, poultry production, farm machinery, pest control, soils, nursery management, conservation, and livestock.

Starting Out

While your college's placement service may be of some help in finding a job, you will need to apply to the director of the extension service at the agricultural college in the state in which you hope to work. If a job vacancy is available, the director of the extension service will screen the qualifications of the various applicants and submit the names to a board or council responsible for making the final selection.

Advancement

Competent consultants, as a rule, are promoted fairly rapidly and early in their careers. The promotions may be in the form of positions of higher responsibility within the same county, reassignment to a different county within the state, or a raise in salary. Many agents, after moving through a succession of more demanding extension jobs, join the staff at the state agricultural college. Many directors of extension services began their careers in this way.

It is also possible to branch out to other areas. Agricultural consultants often go into related jobs, especially those in industries which specialize in agricultural products. The training they have received and their background in agriculture makes them excellent candidates for many jobs in the agricultural industry.

Earnings

The earnings of agricultural consultants vary from state to state and from county to county. Most USDA professionals start out at the GS-5 level (government pay grade) which in 2000 ranged between $21,370 and $27,778 annually, depending on education and experience. Agricultural consultants then move up through the government pay grades, earning more. GS-9 level, for example, had a starting base pay of $32,380 in 2000. With some years of experience with the USDA, and with additional education, consultants can advance to GS-14, which in 2000 paid between $65,983 and $85,774 a year. Most consultants are eligible for other benefits such as paid vacations and sick days, health insurance, and pension plans.

Work Environment

This work is often both mentally and physically taxing. Agricultural consultants will find themselves faced with numerous problems requiring their assistance in the field for long periods of time. They may be in their office handling routine matters every day for a month and then not work in the office for the next six weeks. (Consultants usually have a private office where they can speak in confidence with those who seek assistance.) As a rule, agricultural consultants spend about half of their time in the field working with farmers on specific problems, scheduling or conducting group meetings, or simply distributing new updated information. They usually drive from 500 to 1,500 miles per month while on the job. The work may be hard on the consultant's family, since evening meetings are required, and the agent is often invited to weekend events as well. For example, agents may conduct small informal meetings on Monday and Tuesday nights to discuss particular problems being faced by a small group of farmers in the county. They may be home on Wednesday, work with a student's 4-H Club on Thursday, conduct another meeting on Friday, and then judge a livestock show at the county fair on Saturday.

Hours for consultants are not regular, and the pay is not particularly high considering the number of hours agents are required to work. But this work can be very rewarding. There is great satisfaction to be found working with people who genuinely appreciate the time, advice, and assistance the agent brings.

Outlook

The work of agricultural consultants is, naturally, heavily dependent on the employment of farmers and farm managers. The U.S. Department of Labor predicts a decline in employment for these workers through 2008. As farms consolidate and there are fewer farm families, the need for agricultural consultants may also decline. However, consultants may find opportunities working with rural nonfarming families and various suburban residents who are interested in specialty areas such as urban horticulture and gardening.

As the farming industry is becoming more complex, those consultants with the most thorough education and training will have the best job prospects. The idea of agricultural consulting programs is spreading to many foreign countries. Job opportunities may come from a need for U.S. county and federal agents to assist their counterparts in other countries in setting up and operating agricultural consulting programs.

For More Information

To learn about CSREES and other programs, contact:

U.S. Department of Agriculture
Cooperative State Research, Education and Extension Service (CSREES)
14th Street and Independence Avenue, SW
Washington, DC 20250
Tel: 202-720-2791
Web: http://www.usda.gov

For more information on education and opportunities in the agricultural field, contact:

4-H
Stop 2225
1400 Independence Avenue, SW
Washington, DC 20250-2225
Tel: 202-720-2908
Web: http://www.4h-usa.org

National FFA Organization
6060 FFA Drive
PO Box 68960
Indianapolis, IN 46268
Tel: 317-802-6060
Web: http://www.ffa.org

Agricultural Equipment Technicians

School Subjects

Mathematics
Technical/shop

Personal Skills

Mechanical/manipulative
Technical/scientific

Work Environment

Indoors and outdoors
Primarily multiple locations

Minimum Education Level

Some postsecondary training

Salary Range

$15,000 to $29,315 to $42,000

Certification or Licensing

None available

Outlook

About as fast as the average

Overview

Agricultural equipment technicians work with modern farm machinery. They assemble, adjust, operate, maintain, modify, test, and even help design it. This machinery includes automatic animal feeding systems; milking machine systems; and tilling, planting, harvesting, irrigating, drying, and handling equipment. They work on farms or for agricultural machinery manufacturers or dealerships. They often supervise skilled mechanics and other workers who keep machines and systems operating at maximum efficiency.

History

The history of farming equipment stretches back to prehistoric times when the first agricultural workers developed the sickle. In the Middle Ages, the horse-drawn plow greatly increased farm production, and in the early 1700s,

Jethro Tull designed and built the first mechanical seed planter, further increasing production. The Industrial Revolution brought advances in the design and use of specialized machinery for strenuous and repetitive work. It had a great impact on the agricultural industry, beginning in 1831 with Cyrus McCormick's invention of the reaper.

In the first half of the 20th century, governmental experiment stations developed high-yielding, standardized varieties of farm crops. This, combined with the establishment of agricultural equipment-producing companies, caused a boom in the production of farm machinery. In the late 1930s, the abundance of inexpensive petroleum spurred the development of gasoline- and diesel-run farm machinery. During the early 1940s, the resulting explosion in complex and powerful farm machinery multiplied production and replaced most of the horses and mules used on farms in the United States.

Modern farming is heavily dependent on very complex and expensive machinery. Highly trained and skilled technicians and farm mechanics are therefore required to install, operate, maintain, and modify it, thereby ensuring the nation's farm productivity. Recent developments in agricultural mechanization and automation make the career of agricultural equipment technicians both challenging and rewarding. Sophisticated machines are being used to plant, cultivate, harvest, and process food; to contour, drain, and renovate land; and to clear land and harvest forest products in the process. Qualified agricultural equipment technicians are needed not only to service and sell this equipment, but also to manage it on the farm.

Farming has increasingly become a highly competitive, big business. A successful farmer may have hundreds of thousands or even millions of dollars invested in land and machinery. For this investment to pay off, it is vital to keep the machinery in excellent operating condition. Prompt and reliable service from the farm equipment manufacturer and dealer is necessary for the success of both farmer and dealer. Interruptions or delays because of poor service are costly for everyone involved. To provide good service, manufacturers and dealers need technicians and specialists who possess agricultural and engineering knowledge in addition to technical skills.

The Job

Agricultural equipment technicians work in a wide variety of jobs both on and off the farm. In general, most agricultural equipment technicians find employment in one of three areas: equipment manufacturing, equipment sales and service, and on-farm equipment management.

Equipment manufacturing technicians are involved primarily with the design and testing of agricultural equipment such as farm machinery; irrigation, power, and electrification systems; soil and water conservation equipment; and agricultural harvesting and processing equipment. There are two kinds of technicians working in this field: agricultural engineering technicians and agricultural equipment test technicians.

Agricultural engineering technicians work under the supervision of design engineers. They prepare original layouts and complete detailed drawings of agricultural equipment. They also review plans, diagrams, and blueprints to ensure that new products comply with company standards and design specification. In order to do this they must use their knowledge of biological, engineering, and design principles. They also must keep current on all of the new equipment and materials being developed for the industry to make sure the machines run at their highest capacity.

Agricultural equipment test technicians test and evaluate the performance of agricultural machinery and equipment. In particular, they make sure the equipment conforms with operating requirements, such as horsepower, resistance to vibration, and strength and hardness of parts. They test equipment under actual field conditions on company-operated research farms and under more controlled conditions. They work with test equipment and recording instruments such as bend-fatigue machines, dynamometers, strength testers, hardness meters, analytical balances, and electronic recorders.

Test technicians are also trained in methods of recording the data gathered during these tests. They compute values such as horsepower and tensile strength using algebraic formulas and report their findings using graphs, tables, and sketches.

After the design and testing phases are complete, other agricultural equipment technicians work with engineers to perform any necessary adjustments in the equipment design. By performing these functions under the general supervision of the design engineer, technicians do the engineers' "detective work" so the engineers can devote more time to research and development.

Large agricultural machinery companies may employ agricultural equipment technicians to supervise production, assembly, and plant operations.

Most manufacturers market their products through regional sales organizations to individual dealers. Technicians may serve as *sales representatives* of regional sales offices, where they are assigned a number of dealers in a given territory and sell agricultural equipment directly to them. They may also conduct sales-training programs for the dealers to help them become more effective salespeople.

These technicians are also qualified to work in sales positions within dealerships, either as equipment sales workers or parts clerks. They are required to perform equipment demonstrations for customers. They also appraise the value of used equipment for trade-in allowances. Technicians in these positions may advance to sales or parts manager positions.

Some technicians involved in sales become *systems specialists*, who work for equipment dealerships, assisting farmers in the planning and installation of various kinds of mechanized systems, such as irrigation or materials-handling systems, grain bins, or drying systems.

In the service area, technicians may work as *field service representatives*, forming a liaison between the companies they represent and the dealers. They assist the dealers in product warranty work, diagnose service problems, and give seminars or workshops on new service information and techniques. These types of service technicians may begin their careers as specialists in certain kinds of repairs. *Hydraulic specialists*, for instance, maintain and repair the component parts of hydraulic systems in tractors and other agricultural machines. *Diesel specialists* rebuild, calibrate, and test diesel pumps, injectors, and other diesel engine components.

Many service technicians work as service managers or parts department managers. *Service managers* assign duties to the repair workers, diagnose machinery problems, estimate repair costs for customers, and manage the repair shop.

Parts department managers in equipment dealerships maintain inventories of all the parts that may be requested either by customers or by the service departments of the dealership. They deal directly with customers, parts suppliers, and dealership managers and must have good sales and purchasing skills. They also must be effective business managers.

Technicians working on the farm have various responsibilities, the most important of which is keeping machinery in top working condition during the growing season. During off-season periods they may overhaul or modify equipment or simply keep the machinery in good working order for the next season.

Some technicians find employment as *on-farm machinery managers*, usually working on large farms servicing or supervising the servicing of all automated equipment. They also monitor the field operation of all machines and keep complete records of costs, utilization, and repair procedures relating to the maintenance of each piece of mechanical equipment.

Requirements

High School

You should take as many mathematics courses as you can. You should also take technical/shop and mechanical drawing classes. Take science classes, including courses in earth science, to gain some insight into agriculture, soil conservation, and the environment. Look into adult education programs available to high school students; in such a program, you may be able to enroll in pre-engineering courses.

Postsecondary Training

A high school diploma is necessary, and some college and specialized experience is also important. A four-year education, along with some continuing education courses, can be very helpful in pursuing work, particularly if you're seeking jobs with the government.

Postsecondary education for the agricultural equipment technician should include courses in general agriculture, agricultural power and equipment, practical engineering, hydraulics, agricultural-equipment business methods, electrical equipment, engineering, social science, economics, and sales techniques. On-the-job experience during the summer is invaluable and frequently is included as part of the regular curriculum in these programs. Students are placed on farms, functioning as technicians-in-training. They also may work in farm equipment dealerships where their time is divided between the sales, parts, and service departments. Occupational experience, one of the most important phases of the postsecondary training program, gives students an opportunity to discover which field best suits them and which phase of the business they prefer. Upon completion of this program, most technical and community colleges award an associate's degree.

Other Requirements

The work of the agricultural equipment technician is similar to that of an engineer. You must have a knowledge of physical science and engineering principles and enough mathematical background to work with these principles. You must have a working knowledge of farm crops, machinery, and all agricultural-related products. You should be detail-oriented. You should also have people skills, as you'll be working closely with professionals, other technicians, and farmers.

Exploring

If you live in a farming community, you've probably already had some experience with farming equipment. Vocational agriculture education programs in high schools can be found in most rural settings, many suburban settings, and even in some urban schools. The teaching staff and counselors in these schools can provide considerable information about this career.

Light industrial machinery is now used in almost every industry. It is always helpful to watch machinery being used and to talk with people who own, operate, and repair it.

Summer and part-time work on a farm, in an agricultural equipment manufacturing plant, or in an equipment sales and service business offers opportunities to work on or near agricultural and light industrial machinery. Such a job may provide a clearer idea about the various activities, challenges, rewards, and possible limitations of this career.

Employers

Depending on their area of specialization, agricultural equipment technicians work for engineers, manufacturers, scientists, sales and services companies, and farmers. They can also find work with government agencies, such as the U.S. Department of Agriculture and the Agriculture Research Service.

Starting Out

It is still possible to enter this career by starting as an inexperienced worker in a machinery manufacturer's plant or on a farm and learning machine technician skills on the job. However, this approach is becoming increasingly difficult due to the complexity of modern machinery. Because of this, some formal classroom training is usually necessary, and many people find it difficult to complete even part-time study of the field's theory and science while also working a full-time job.

The demand for qualified agricultural equipment technicians currently exceeds the supply. Operators and managers of large, well-equipped farms and farm equipment companies in need of employees keep in touch with colleges offering agricultural equipment programs. Students who do well during their occupational experience period usually have an excellent chance of going to work for the same employer after graduation. Many colleges have an interview day on which personnel representatives of manufacturers, distributors, farm owners or managers, and dealers are invited to recruit students completing technician programs. In general, any student who does well in a training program can expect employment immediately upon graduation.

Advancement

Opportunities for advancement and self-employment are excellent for those with the initiative to keep abreast of continuing developments in the farm equipment field. Technicians often attend company schools in sales and service or take advanced evening courses in colleges.

Earnings

Agricultural technicians working for the government may be able to enter a position at GS-5 (government wage scale), which was $21,370 in 2000. Those with more education and specialized experience may be able to enter at GS-8—$29,315. The Bureau of Labor Statistics lists the weekly median wage of engineering and related technologists and technicians as $616 in 1998. Those working on farms often receive room and board as a supplement to their annual salary. The salary that technicians eventually receive depends—as do most salaries—on individual ability, initiative, and the supply of skilled technicians in the field of work or locality. There is opportunity to work overtime during planting and harvesting seasons.

In addition to their salaries, most technicians receive fringe benefits such as health and retirement packages, paid vacations, and other benefits similar to those received by engineering technicians. Technicians employed in sales are usually paid a commission in addition to their base salary.

Work Environment

Working conditions vary according to the type of field chosen. The technician who is a part of a large farming operation will work indoors or outdoors depending on the season and the tasks that need to be done. Planning machine overhauls and the directing of such work usually are done in enclosed spaces equipped for such work. As implied by its name, field servicing and repairs are done in the field.

Some agricultural equipment sales representatives work in their own or nearby communities, while others must travel extensively.

Technicians in agricultural equipment research, development, and production usually work under typical factory conditions: some work in an office or laboratory; others in a manufacturing plant; or, in some cases, field testing and demonstration are performed where the machinery will be used.

For technicians who assemble, adjust, modify, or test equipment and for those who provide customer service, application studies, and maintenance services, the surroundings may be similar to large automobile service centers.

In all cases, safety precautions must be a constant concern. Appropriate clothing, an acute awareness of one's environment, and careful lifting or hoisting of heavy machinery must be standard. While safety practices have improved greatly over the years, certain risks do exist. Heavy lifting may cause injury, and burns and cuts are always possible. The surroundings may be noisy and grimy. Some work is performed in cramped or awkward physical positions. Gasoline fumes and odors from oil products are a constant factor. Most technicians ordinarily work a 40-hour week, but emergency repairs may require overtime.

Outlook

The *Occupational Outllook Handbook* reports that employment of farm equipment mechanics is expected to decline. However, agricultural equipment businesses now demand more expertise than ever before. A variety of complex specialized machines and mechanical devices are steadily being produced and modified to help farmers improve the quality and productivity of their labor. These machines require trained technicians to design, produce, test, sell, and service them. Trained workers also are needed to instruct the final owners in their proper repair, operation, and maintenance.

In addition, the agricultural industry is adopting advanced computer and electronic technology. Computer skills are becoming more and more useful in this field. Precision farming will also require specialized training as agricultural equipment becomes hooked up to satellite systems.

As agriculture becomes more technical, the agricultural equipment technician will assume an increasingly vital role in helping farmers solve problems that interfere with efficient production. These opportunities exist not only in the United States, but also worldwide. As agricultural economies everywhere become mechanized, inventive technicians with training in modern business principles will find expanding employment opportunities abroad.

For More Information

To read equipment sales statistics, agricultural reports, and other news of interest to agricultural equipment technicians, visit the EMI Web site.

Equipment Manufacturers Institute (EMI)
10 South Riverside Plaza
Chicago, IL 60606-3710
Tel: 312-321-1470
Email: emi@emi.org
Web: http://www.emi.org

At the FEMA Web site, you can learn about their publications and read industry news.

Farm Equipment Manufacturers Association (FEMA)
1000 Executive Parkway, Suite 100
St. Louis, MO 63141-6369
Tel: 314-878-2304
Web: http://www.farmequip.org

Agricultural Pilots

School Subjects
Mathematics
Physics

Personal Skills
Leadership/management
Technical/scientific

Work Environment
Indoors and outdoors
Primarily multiple locations

Minimum Education Level
Some postsecondary training

Salary Range
$25,000 to $30,000 to $80,000

Certification or Licensing
Required by all states

Outlook
Little change or more slowly than the average

Overview

Agricultural pilots, also called ag pilots, perform flying jobs related to the farming industry. They are skilled professionals who operate aircraft for such purposes as transporting cargo to market, aerial applications (also known as crop dusting), hauling feed, or planting seed. In addition to flying aircraft, agricultural pilots are responsible for performing a variety of safety-related tasks involving both the aircraft and the cargo. They may be self-employed or work for large pest control companies or government agencies.

History

The history of agricultural aviation is, naturally, tied to that of modern aviation. This period is generally considered to have begun with the flight of Orville and Wilbur Wright's heavier-than-air machine on December 17, 1903. On that day, the Wright brothers flew their machine four times and became the first airplane pilots. In the early days of aviation, the pilot's job was quite different from that of the pilot of today. As he flew the plane, for example, Orville Wright was lying on his stomach in the middle of the bottom wing of the plane. There was a strap across his hips, and to turn the plane, he had to tilt his hips from side to side—hardly the way today's pilot makes a turn!

The aviation industry developed rapidly as designers raced to improve upon the Wright brothers' design. During the early years of flight, many aviators earned a living as "barnstormers," entertaining people with stunts and by taking passengers on short flights around the countryside. As airplanes became more dependable, they were adapted for a variety of purposes such as use in the military and for the United States government-run air mail service. According to the National Agricultural Aviation Association, the first time a plane was used to spread pesticide was in 1921. In an experiment conducted by the military, lead arsenate dust was spread by plane to stop a moth infestation in Ohio. By 1923 crop dusting was being done on a commercial basis.

Today planes used for agricultural aviation are specifically designed for that purpose. They can carry hundreds of gallons of pesticides and are equipped with the latest technology, such as Global Positioning System (GPS). Unlike the crop-dusting process of the past, which used dry chemicals, today's process typically involves liquid pesticides and other controlling products as well as nutrition sprays. Advances in agricultural aviation have allowed U.S. farms to become increasingly productive.

The Job

Agricultural pilots perform a number of duties that benefit the farming industry as well as the environment. They assist farmers in the prevention of crop damage, among other duties performed. Some work for pest control companies while others are self-employed. In farm work, agricultural pilots spray chemicals over crops and orchards to fertilize them, control plant diseases or weeds, and control pests. They also drop seeds into fields to grow crops.

Before agricultural pilots begin the process of spraying farmland, they must survey the area for buildings, hills, power lines, and other obstacles and hazards. They must also notify residents and businesses in the general area that they will spray so that people and animals can be moved away from target areas.

Some agricultural pilots, particularly those who work for pest control companies, may mix their own chemicals, using their knowledge of what mixture may be best for certain types of plants, plant or soil conditions, or pest problems. Agricultural pilots fly small, turboprop planes, which are slower compared to larger, transport craft, but which are good for flying close to the ground and for carrying heavy loads. They must fly close to the ground, often only a few feet above a crop, so that they will only hit designated areas with the chemicals.

Agricultural pilots help farmers by dropping food over pastures. They may photograph wildlife or count game animals for conservation programs. And their work also extends into forests, fields, and swamps, where herbicides and insecticides are needed. They also fight forest fires by dumping water or fire retardant materials over burning areas.

No matter what the job, pilots must determine weather and flight conditions, make sure that sufficient fuel is on board to complete the flight safely, and verify the maintenance status of the airplane before each flight. They perform system checks to test the proper functioning of instrumentation and electronic and mechanical systems on the plane.

Once all of these preflight duties are done, the pilot taxis the aircraft to the designated runway and prepares for takeoff. Takeoff speeds must be calculated based on the aircraft's weight, which is affected by the weight of the cargo being carried.

During flights, agricultural pilots must constantly be aware of their surroundings since they fly so close to the ground and frequently are near hazards such as power lines. They need good judgment to deal with any emergency situations that might arise. They monitor aircraft systems, keep an eye on the weather conditions, and perform the job of the flight, such as spraying fertilizer.

Once the pilot has landed and taxied to the appropriate area, he or she follows a "shutdown" checklist of procedures. Pilots also keep logs of their flight hours. Those who are self-employed or working for smaller companies are typically responsible for refueling the airplane, performing maintenance, and keeping business records.

Requirements

High School

There are a number of classes you can take in high school to help prepare you for becoming a pilot. You should take science classes, such as chemistry and physics, as well as mathematics, such as algebra and geometry. Take computer classes to familiarize yourself with this tool. Since you will be responsible for the maintenance and care of a plane, you may also benefit from taking an electronics shop class or other shop class where you get to work on engines. Take English classes to improve your research and writing skills. Throughout your career you will need to study flying or repair manuals, file reports, and communicate with customers. Since you may be responsible for record keeping, take business or accounting classes. If your school offers agriculture classes, take any that will teach you about soils, crops, and growing methods.

Postsecondary Training

Many companies that employ pilots prefer to hire candidates with at least two years of college training. Courses in engineering, meteorology, physics, mathematics, and agriculture are helpful in preparing for this career. In addition to these courses, you will need training as a pilot. There are approximately 600 civilian flying schools certified by the Federal Aviation Administration (FAA), including some colleges and universitites that offer degree credit for pilot training. A number of schools offer training specifically in agricultural aviation. Some people take up this career after leaving the military, where they trained as pilots.

Certification or Licensing

Agricultural pilots must hold a commercial pilot's license from the FAA. A fairly long and rigorous process is involved in obtaining a commercial license. The first step in this process is to receive flying instruction. Anyone who is 16 or over and can pass a rigid mandatory physical exam can apply for permission to take flying lessons. When you have finished this training, you can take a written exam. If you pass the exam and fulfill such requirements as being at least 17 years of age and have completed a solo flying requirement of 20 hours or more, you can apply for your private pilot's license. The next step in getting a commercial license is to continue to log flying time and increase your knowledge and skills. To receive your commercial license you must be at least 18 years of age, have 250 hours of flying time, and successfully complete a number of exams. These tests include a physical exam; a written test given by the FAA covering such topics as safe flight operations, navigation principles, and federal aviation regulations; and a practical test to demonstrate your flying skills. Pilots must also receive a rating for the kind of plane they can fly (such as single-engine or multiengine). In addition, a commercial pilot needs an instrument rating by the

FAA and a restricted radio telephone operator's permit by the Federal Communications Commission. In states where they spray restricted pesticides, agricultural pilots must be certified by the U.S. Department of Agriculture.

Other Requirements

All pilots must have sound physical and emotional health. They need excellent eyesight and eye-hand coordination as well as excellent hearing and normal heart rate and blood pressure. The successful agricultural pilot is also detail-oriented since much paperwork, planning, and following of regulations is involved in this job. Those who are self-employed or working for smaller companies may find that they have frequent contact with customers, and so they must be able to work well with others. Naturally, an agricultural pilot should have an interest in farming methods and the environment as well as a love of flying. Good judgment is essential for this work.

Exploring

You can explore this field through a number of activities. Join groups such as your high school aviation club and the National FFA Organization (formerly Future Farmers of America). These groups may give you the opportunity to meet with professionals in the field, learn about farm products and management, and find others with similar interests. Read publications related to these industries such as the magazines *AgAir Update* and *Progressive Farmer*. If you have the financial resources, you can take flying lessons once you are 16 and have passed a physical exam. Also, consider learning how to operate a ham radio. This skill will help you when you apply for your restricted radio operator's permit, a requirement for commercial pilots.

Employers

California and the southern states, where the crop growing season lasts longest, are where agricultural pilots find the most work. They also find some work with northern crops and in forests of the northeastern and western states. Many are employed by crop dusting companies, while others are self-employed. Federal and state government departments also employ agricultural pilots to assist with environmental, conservation, and preservation needs.

Starting Out

It is not unusual for people to enter this field after gaining experience in the agricultural industry itself, working on farms and learning about crop production while they also develop their flying skills. Others enter with flying as their first love and are drawn to the challenge of agricultural aviation. Once pilots have completed their training, they may find that contacts made through aviation schools lead to job openings. Those who have the financial means can begin by opening their own business. Equipment, however, is very expensive—a single plane appropriately outfitted can cost anywhere from $100,000 to $900,000. A number of people, therefore, begin by working for large aerial applications companies before they strike out on their own.

Advancement

Agricultural pilots who work for a company can be promoted to manager. Self-employed agricultural pilots move up by charging more money for their services and increasing their client base. Another way to advance is to work in other areas of commercial aviation. These pilots may fly cargo and people to remote locations or become aerial photographers.

Earnings

If they work throughout the entire year, agricultural pilots can make between $30,000 and $80,000 per year. Those who fly about half the year make near $25,000. Agricultural pilots who are employed by companies rarely get paid vacation and only a few companies offer health and accident insurance and profit-sharing and pension plans.

Work Environment

The vast majority of an agricultural pilot's job takes place outdoors, during the early morning and early evening hours. Their work is demanding and can be hazardous. When flying, agricultural pilots wear safety gear consisting of a helmet, safety belt, and shoulder harness, because they fly under such difficult conditions. They fly close to the ground in populated areas and must be cautious to avoid obstacles. They also face exposure to pesticides and other harsh substances. When mixing or loading chemicals onto the plane, they sometimes wear gloves or masks to prevent the inhaling of harmful vapors.

Outlook

Employment opportunities for experienced agricultural pilots are expected to continue into the future. However, the demand for agricultural pilots depends largely on farmers' needs. For example, during times when insect and pest control becomes a problem, there is greater demand for agricultural pilots. There is also some concern within the industry that genetically engineered crops (resistant to certain diseases) may decrease the need for aerial applications and cause a loss of business for agricultural pilots. Keeping these factors in mind, employment prospects will probably be best with larger farms and ranches and in states with long growing seasons.

For More Information

This organization has information on crop protection products and developments in the industry.

American Crop Protection Association
1156 Fifteenth Street, NW, Suite 400
Washington, DC 20005
Tel: 202-296-1585
Web: http://www.acpa.org

This organization promotes high standards and continuing education in the field.

National Agricultural Aviation Association
1005 E Street, SE
Washington, DC 20003
Tel: 202-546-5722
Email: information@agaviation.org
Web: http://www.agaviation.org

For information on opportunities in the agricultural field and local chapters, contact:

National FFA Organization
6060 FFA Drive
PO Box 68960
Indianapolis, IN 46268
Tel: 317-802-6060
Web: http://www.ffa.org

These magazines, available in print, also have Web sites with feature articles and information related to their fields.

AgAir Update
PO Box 1548
Perry, GA 31069
Tel: 912-987-2250
Web: http://www.agairupdate.com

Progressive Farmer
PO Box 830656
Birmingham, AL 35283
Tel: 800-292-2340
Web: http://www.progressivefarmer.com

Agricultural Scientists

School Subjects

Biology
Chemistry

Personal Skills

Communication/ideas
Technical/scientific

Work Environment

Indoors and outdoors
Primarily multiple locations

Minimum Education Level

Bachelor's degree

Salary Range

$24,200 to $42,340 to $79,820+

Certification or Licensing

Voluntary

Outlook

About as fast as the average

Overview

Agricultural scientists study all aspects of living organisms and the relationships of plants and animals to their environment. They conduct basic research in laboratories or in the field. They apply the results to such tasks as increasing crop yields and improving the environment. Some agricultural scientists plan and administer programs for testing foods, drugs, and other products. Others direct activities at public exhibits at such places as zoos or botanical gardens. Some agricultural scientists are professors at colleges and universities or work as consultants to business firms or the government. Others work in technical sales and service jobs for manufacturers of agricultural products. There are approximately 21,000 agricultural scientists in the United States.

History

In 1840, Justius von Liebig of Germany published *Organic Chemistry in Its Applications to Agriculture and Physiology* and launched the systematic development of the agricultural sciences. A formal system of agricultural education soon followed in both Europe and the United States. Prior to the publication of this work, agricultural developments relied on the collected experiences of farmers handed down over generations. Agricultural science has techniques in common with many other disciplines including biology, botany, genetics, nutrition, breeding, and engineering. Discoveries and improvements in these fields contributed to advances in agriculture. Some milestones include the discovery of the practice of crop rotation and the application of manure as fertilizer, which greatly increased farm yields in the 1700s. Farm mechanization was greatly advanced by the invention of the mechanical reaper in 1831 and the gasoline tractor in 1892. Chemical fertilizers were first used in the 19th century; pesticides and herbicides soon followed. In 1900, the research of a 19th-century Austrian monk, Gregor Johann Mendel, was rediscovered. He used generations of garden peas to test his theories that formed the foundation for the science of genetics.

In the 20th century, scientists and engineers were at the forefront of farm, crop, and food processing improvements. Conservationist Gifford Pinchot developed some of the first methods to prevent soil erosion in 1910, and Clarence Birdseye perfected a method of freezing food in the 1920s. Birdseye's discoveries allowed for whole new crops of produce previously too perishable for the marketplace. Engineers in the 1930s developed more powerful farm machinery, and scientists developed hybrid corn; by the 1960s, high-powered machinery, and better quality feed and pesticides were in common use. Today, advances in genetic engineering and biotechnology are leading to more efficient, economical methods of farming, and more markets for crops.

The Job

The nature of the work of the agricultural scientist can be broken down into several areas of specialization. Within each specialization there are various careers.

The following are careers that fall under the areas of plant and soil science.

Agronomists investigate large-scale food-crop problems, conduct experiments, and develop new methods of growing crops to ensure more efficient production, higher yields, and improved quality. They use genetic engineering to develop crops that are resistant to pests, drought, and plant diseases.

Agronomists also engage in soil science. They analyze soils to find ways to increase production and reduce soil erosion. They study the responses of various soil types to fertilizers, tillage practices, and crop rotation. Since soil science is related to environmental science, agronomists may also use their expertise to consult with farmers and agricultural companies on environmental quality and effective land use.

Botanists are concerned with plants and their environment, structure, heredity, and economic value in such fields as agronomy, horticulture, and medicine.

Horticulturists study fruit and nut orchards as well as garden plants such as vegetables and flowers. They conduct experiments to develop new and improved varieties and to increase crop quality and yields. They also work to improve plant culture methods for the landscaping and beautification of communities, parks, and homes.

Plant breeders apply genetics and biotechnology to improve plants' yield, quality, and resistance to harsh weather, disease, and insects. They might work on developing strains of wild or cultivated plants that will have a larger yield and increase profits.

Plant pathologists research plant diseases and the decay of plant products to identify symptoms, determine causes, and develop control measures. They attempt to predict outbreaks by studying how different soils, climates, and geography affect the spread and intensity of plant disease.

Another area of specialization for agricultural scientists is animal science.

Animal scientists conduct research and develop improved methods for housing, breeding, feeding, and controlling diseases of domestic farm animals. They inspect and grade livestock food products, purchase livestock, or work in sales and marketing of livestock products. They often consult agricultural businesses on such areas as upgrading animal housing, lowering mortality rates, or increasing production of animal products such as milk and eggs.

Dairy scientists study the selection, breeding, feeding, and management of dairy cattle. For example, they research how various types of food and environmental conditions affect milk production and quality. They also develop new breeding programs to improve dairy herds.

Poultry scientists study the breeding, feeding, and management of poultry to improve the quantity and quality of eggs and other poultry products.

Animal breeders specialize in improving the quality of farm animals. They may work for a state agricultural department, agricultural extension station, or university. Some of their work is done in a laboratory, but much of it is done outdoors working directly on animals. Using their knowledge of genetics, animal breeders develop systems for animals to achieve desired characteristics such as strength, fast maturation, resistance to disease, and quality of meat.

Food science is a specialty closely related to animal science, but it focuses on meeting consumer demand for food products in ways that are healthy, safe, and convenient. *Food scientists* use their backgrounds in chemistry, microbiology, and other sciences to develop new or better ways of preserving, packaging, processing, storing, and delivering foods. *Food technologists* work in product development to discover new food sources and analyze food content to determine levels of vitamins, fat, sugar, and protein. Food technologists also work to enforce government regulations, inspecting food processing areas and ensuring that sanitation, safety, quality, and waste management standards are met.

Another field related to agricultural science is agricultural engineering. *Agricultural engineers* apply engineering principles to work in the food and agriculture industries. They design or develop agricultural equipment and machines, supervise production, and conduct tests on new designs and machine parts. They develop plans and specifications for agricultural buildings and for drainage and irrigation systems. They work on flood control, soil erosion, and land reclamation projects. They design food processing systems and equipment to convert farm products to consumer foods. Agricultural engineers contribute to making farming easier and more profitable through the introduction of new farm machinery and through advancements in soil and water conservation. Agricultural engineers in industry may be engaged in research or in the design, testing, or sales of equipment. Much of the research conducted by agricultural scientists is done in laboratories and requires a familiarity with research techniques and the use of laboratory equipment and computers. Some research, however, is carried out wherever necessary. A botanist may have occasion to examine the plants that grow in the volcanic valleys of Alaska, or an animal breeder may study the behavior of animals on the plains of Africa.

Requirements

High School

Follow your high school's college preparatory program, which will include courses in English, foreign language, mathematics, and government. Also take biology, chemistry, physics, and any other science courses available. You must also become familiar with basic computer skills, including programming. It may be possible for you to perform laboratory assistant duties for your science teachers. Visiting research laboratories and attending lectures by agricultural scientists can also be helpful.

Postsecondary Training

Educational requirements for agricultural scientists are very high. A doctorate is usually mandatory for careers as college or university professors, independent researchers, or field managers. A bachelor's degree may be acceptable for some entry-level jobs, such as testing or inspecting technicians, or as technical sales or service representatives. Promotions, however, are very limited for these employees unless they earn advanced degrees.

To become an agricultural scientist, you should pursue a degree related to agricultural and biological science. As an undergraduate, you should have a firm foundation in biology, with courses in chemistry, physics, mathematics, and English. Most colleges and universities have agricultural science curriculums, although liberal arts colleges may emphasize the biological sciences. State universities usually offer agricultural science programs, too.

While pursuing an advanced degree, you'll participate in research projects and write a dissertation on your specialized area of study. You'll also do fieldwork and laboratory research along with your classroom studies.

Certification or Licensing

Agricultural scientists can be listed in the American Registry of Certified Professionals in Agronomy, Crops, and Soils. To qualify for certification, you must earn a bachelor's degree and work five years in the field. Those with advanced degrees can qualify with less experience.

Other Requirements

As a researcher, you should be self-motivated enough to work effectively alone, yet be able to function cooperatively as part of a team. You should have an inexhaustible curiosity about the nature of living things and their environment. You must be systematic in your work habits and in your approach to investigation and experimentation and must have the persistence to continue or start over when experiments are not immediately successful.

Work performed by agricultural scientists in offices and laboratories requires intense powers of concentration and the ability to communicate one's thoughts systematically. In addition to these skills, physical stamina is necessary for those scientists who do field research in remote areas of the world.

Exploring

If you live in an agricultural community, you may be able to find part-time or summer work on a farm or ranch. The 4-H Club and the National FFA Organization (formerly Future Farmers of America) offer programs that can introduce you to the concerns of farmers and researchers, and may involve you directly in science projects. Contact your county's extension office to learn about regional projects. You may also find part-time work in veterinarian's offices, florist shops, landscape nurseries, orchards, farms, zoos, aquariums, botanical gardens, and museums. Volunteer work is often available in zoos and animal shelters.

Employers

About 40 percent of all agricultural scientists work for federal, state, and local governments. They work within the U.S. Department of Agriculture and the Environmental Protection Agency, and for regional extension agencies and soil conservation departments. Scientists with doctorates may work on the faculty of colleges and universities. Researchers work for chemical and pharmaceutical companies, and agribusiness and consulting firms. Agricultural scientists also work in the food processing industry.

Starting Out

Agricultural scientists often are recruited prior to graduation. College or university placement offices are a source of information about jobs, and students may arrange interviews with recruiters who visit the campus.

Direct application may be made to the personnel departments of colleges and universities, private industries, or nonprofit research foundations. People interested in positions with the federal government may contact the local offices of state employment services and the U.S. Office of Personnel Management or the Federal Job Information Centers, which are located in various large cities throughout the country. Private employment agencies are another method that might be considered. Large companies sometimes conduct job fairs in major cities and will advertise them in the business sections of the local newspapers.

Advancement

Advancement in this field depends on education, experience, and job performance. Agricultural scientists with advanced degrees generally start in teaching or research and advance to administrative and management positions, such as supervisor of a research program. The number of such jobs is limited, however, and often the route to advancement is through specialization. The narrower specialties are often the most valuable.

People who enter this field with only a bachelor's degree are much more restricted. After starting in testing and inspecting jobs or as technical sales and service representatives, they may progress to advanced technicians, particularly in medical research, or become high school biology teachers. In the latter case, they must have had courses in education and meet the state requirements for teachers.

Earnings

According to the U.S. Department of Labor, the median annual salaries of agricultural scientists (from all specialty areas) was approximately $42,340 in 1998. The lowest paid 10 percent (which generally included those just starting out in the field) earned roughly $24,200, while the highest paid 10 percent made approximately $79,820 or more per year. In 1999 the U.S. Department of Labor also recorded a salary breakdown by specialty for those working for the federal government in nonsupervisory, supervisory, and managerial roles. The breakdown included the following: the average annual salary for those working in animal science was $69,400; for those working in soil science, $53,600; and for those working in horticulture, $53,800.

Unless you're hired for just a short-term project, you'll likely receive health and retirement benefits in addition to your annual salary.

Work Environment

Agricultural scientists work regular hours, although researchers often choose to work longer when their experiments have reached critical points. Competition in the research field may be stiff, causing a certain amount of stress.

Agricultural scientists generally work in offices, laboratories, or classrooms where the environment is clean, healthy, and safe. Some agricultural scientists such as botanists periodically take field trips where living facilities may be primitive and strenuous physical activity may be required.

Outlook

The employment outlook for agricultural scientists looks good and is expected to grow about as fast as the average through 2008. Naturally, those with doctorates and the most experience will have the best opportunities; however, those with bachelor's and master's degrees will also find work as technicians or in farm management.

The fields of biotechnology and genetics may hold the best opportunities for agricultural scientists. New developments, such as methods of processing corn for use in medicines, will alter the marketplace. Scientists will also be actively involved in improving both the environmental impact of farming, as well as crop yields, as they focus on methods of decontaminating soil, protecting ground water, crop rotation, and other efforts of conservation. Scientists will also have the challenge of promoting these new methods to farmers.

For More Information

To learn about opportunities for scientists in the dairy industry and the association's student division, contact:

American Dairy Science Association
1111 North Dunlap Avenue
Savoy, IL 61874
Tel: 217-356-3182
Email: adsa@assochq.org
Web: http://www.adsa.uiuc.edu

To learn about benefits for engineers, as well as the association's student competitions and scholarships, contact:

American Society of Agricultural Engineering
2950 Niles Road
St. Joseph, MI 49085-9659
Tel: 616-429-0300
Email: hq@asae.org
Web: http://asae.org

For the free career resource guide, **Exploring Careers in Agronomy, Crops, Soils, and Environmental Sciences,** *contact:*

American Society of Agronomy
677 South Segoe Road
Madison, WI 53711
Tel: 608-273-8080
Web: http://www.agronomy.org

For more information on education and opportunities in the agricultural field, contact:

4-H
Stop 2225
1400 Independence Avenue, SW
Washington, DC 20250-2225
Tel: 202-720-2908
Web: http://www.4h-usa.org

National FFA Organization
6060 FFA Drive
PO Box 68960
Indianapolis, IN 46268
Tel: 317-802-6060
Web: http://www.ffa.org

Animal Breeders and Technicians

School Subjects
Biology
Business

Personal Skills
Following instructions
Technical/scientific

Work Environment
Indoors and outdoors
Primarily one location

Minimum Education Level
High school diploma

Salary Range
$15,000 to $25,000 to $35,000

Certification or Licensing
Voluntary

Outlook
About as fast as the average

Overview

Animal breeders and technicians help breed, raise, and market a variety of animals: cattle, sheep, pigs, horses, mules, and poultry for livestock; pets such as canaries, parrots, dogs, and cats; and other more exotic animals such as ostriches, alligators, minks, and many zoo animals. Technicians who are primarily involved with the breeding and feeding of animals are sometimes referred to as *animal husbandry technicians*.

In general, animal breeders and technicians are concerned with the propagation, feeding, housing, health, production, and marketing of animals. These technicians work in many different settings and capacities: they may supervise unskilled farm workers; serve as *field representatives* assisting in the sales of animals to customers; work in kennels, stables, ranches, or zoos reproducing species and breeds for other clients or their own organization; or work on their own on a particular breed of interest. The diversity of employment available for well-trained and well-qualified animal breeders and technicians makes this career extremely flexible. As science progresses, opportunities for these technicians should broaden.

History

Breeding animals has been part of raising livestock since animals were first domesticated. With the discovery of genetics, the science behind the breeding selection became more exact. Great shifts can be made in a species with genetically selected breeding programs. All domesticated dogs extend from a precursor to the modern wolf. So even though miniature poodles and St. Bernards have extremely different appearances and are seemingly incompatible, they are actually so closely related genetically that they can reproduce with each other.

Farm animals have been bred to increase meat on the animal, increase production of eggs and milk, and increase resistance to disease. Both pets and farm animals have been bred for appearance, with show animals produced in almost every domesticated species.

As regions specialized in certain breeds, organizations developed to recognize and register them, eventually developing standards for accepted breeds. Organizations such as the American Kennel Club establish criteria by which species are judged, and the criteria can be quite specific. For example, dog breeds have specific ranges of height, shoulder width, fur color, arch of leg, and such, and any dog outside the variance cannot be shown in competition. This is partly to ensure that the species is bred by trained and informed individuals, and to keep the breed from inadvertently shifting over time. Breeds, however, can be intentionally shifted, and this is how new breeds begin.

Until the end of the 20th century, breeding was controlled by reproduction through mating pairs, whether through natural or artificial insemination. Recently, however, there has been a radical breakthrough in cloning, where the gene pool of the offspring remains identical to the parent cloned. Although this work is extremely costly and experimental, it is expected to change the range of work that breeders can do in reproduction.

The Job

Most animal breeders and technicians work as *livestock production technicians* with cattle, sheep, swine, or horses; or as poultry production technicians, with chickens, turkeys, geese, or ducks. Other animal breeders work with domesticated animals kept as pets, such as song birds, parrots, and all dog and cat breeds. Even wildlife populations that are kept in reserves, ranches, zoos, or aquariums are bred with the guidance of a breeder or technician. Each category of animal (such as birds), family (parrot), species (African gray parrot), and even some individual breeds within a category have technicians working on their reproduction if they are bred for livestock or domestic use. Within each of these categories the jobs may be specialized for one aspect of the animal's reproductive cycle.

For example, technicians and breeders who work in food-source bird production can be divided into specific areas of concentration. In breeding-flock production, technicians may work as *farm managers*, directing the operation of one or more farms. They may be *flock supervisors* with five or six assistants working directly with farmers under contract to produce hatching eggs. On pedigree breeding farms, technicians may oversee all the people who transport, feed, and care for the poultry. Technicians in breeding-flock production seek ways to improve efficiency in the use of time, materials, and labor; they also strive to make maximum effective use of data-processing equipment.

Technicians in hatchery management operate and maintain the incubators and hatchers, where eggs develop as embryos. These technicians must be trained in incubation, sexing, grading, scheduling, and effectively using available technology. The egg processing phase begins when the eggs leave the farm. *Egg processing technicians* handle egg pickup, trucking, delivery, and quality control. With experience, technicians in this area can work as supervisors and plant managers. These technicians need training in egg processing machinery and refrigeration equipment.

Technicians in poultry meat production oversee the production, management, and inspection of birds bred specifically for consumption as meat. Technicians may work directly with flocks or in supervisory positions.

Poultry husbandry technicians conduct research in breeding, feeding, and management of poultry. They examine selection and breeding practices in order to increase efficiency of production and to improve the quality of poultry products.

Egg candlers inspect eggs to determine quality and fitness for incubation according to prescribed standards. They check to see if eggs have been fertilized and if they are developing correctly.

Some poultry technicians also work as *field-contact technicians*, inspecting poultry farms for food processing companies. They ensure that growers maintain contract standards for feeding and housing birds and controlling disease. They tour barns, incubation units, and related facilities to observe sanitation and weather protection provisions. Field-contact technicians ensure that specific grains are administered according to schedules, inspect birds for evidence of disease, and weigh them to determine growth rates.

For other livestock, the categories are similar, as are the range of jobs. For nonfarm animals, the average breeder works with several animals within a breed or species to produce offspring for sale. Although there are ranches that produce a large number of exotic animals, and some stables and kennels that run full-staff breeding operations, most breeders for pets work out of their homes, with animals that they appreciate. There are also production shops, usually referred to as puppy mills, that produce pets for sale, but do so without much regard to the quality or well-being of the animals they are producing. Dismissed as unprofessional by established breeders and usually challenged by local authorities for quality of care provided to the animals, these are commonly not reputable enterprises, although they may be profitable in the short-term.

One area of animal production technology that merits special mention because of the increasing focus on its use in animal husbandry is that of artificial breeding. Three kinds of technicians working in this specialized area of animal production are artificial-breeding technicians, artificial-breeding laboratory technicians, and artificial insemination technicians.

Artificial breeding can be differentiated by the goal of the breeder: food (poultry and cattle), sport (horses and dogs), conservation (endangered species kept in captivity), and science (mice, rabbits, monkeys, and any other animals used for research). Breeders work to create better, stronger breeds of animals or to maintain good existing breeds.

Because of the increasing cost of shipping adult animals from location to location to keep the gene pool diverse in a species or breed, animal breeders have developed successful methods of shipping frozen semen to allow breeding across distances. For zoo animals such as the elephant, rhinoceros, and hippopotamus, this has allowed zoos to build their populations with good genetic diversity without the overwhelming difficulty of transporting a several-thousand-pound male over expressways to attempt breeding with a new female to which he may or may not be attracted. Because semen can be examined microscopically, the technician is able to eliminate problem samples before insemination occurs.

Artificial-breeding technicians collect and package semen for use in insemination. They examine the semen under a microscope to determine density and motility of sperm cells, and they dilute the semen according to standard formulas. They transfer the semen to shipping and storage containers with identifying data such as the source, date taken, and quality. They also keep records related to all of their activities. In some cases they may also be responsible for inseminating the females.

Artificial-breeding laboratory technicians handle the artificial insemination of all kinds of animals, but most often these technicians specialize in the laboratory aspects of the activity. They measure purity, potency, and density of animal semen and add extenders and antibiotics to it. They keep records, clean and sterilize laboratory equipment, and perform experimental tests to develop improved methods of processing and preserving semen.

Artificial insemination technicians do exactly what their name implies: they collect semen from the male species of an animal and artificially inseminate the female. *Poultry inseminators* collect semen from roosters and fertilize hens' eggs. They examine the roosters' semen for quality and density, measure specified amounts of semen for loading into inseminating guns, inject semen into hens, and keep accurate records of all aspects of the operation. This area of animal production is expected to grow as poultry production expands.

Whether the breeding is done artificially or naturally, the goals are the same. *Cattle breeders* mate males and females to produce animals with preferred traits such as leaner meat and less fat. It is desirable to produce cows who give birth easily and are less susceptible to illness than the average cow. In artificial insemination, cows are inseminated with a gun, much like hens, which allows for many animals to be bred from the sperm of one male. By repeating the process of artificial breeding for many generations, a more perfect animal can be produced.

Horse breeders and *dog breeders* strive to create more physically and physiologically desirable animals. They want horses and dogs who perform well, move fast, and look beautiful. Longer legs and shinier coats are examples of desirable show traits for these animals. Temperament is another quality considered in reproduction and is one of the traits that a good breeder can work for, although it is not directly linked to a specific gene.

Some breeders produce many small animals such as mice, rabbits, dogs, and cats. These animals can be used in scientific research. For example, some laboratories raise thousands of mice to be used in experiments. These mice are shipped all over the world so that scientists can study them.

Animals raised for fur or skin also require extensive technological assistance. Mink farms, ostrich farms, and alligator farms are animal production industries that need husbandry, feeding, and health technicians. As the popularity of one species rises or falls, others replace it, and new animal specialists are needed.

For all breeders, it is essential that they keep track of the lineage of the animals they breed. The genetic history for at least three previous generations is usually considered the minimum background required to ensure no inbreeding. For animals sold as pedigreed, these records are certified by some overseeing organizations. For animals being bred from wildlife stock, purity of the genetic line within a breed or species is required before an animal is allowed to reproduce. Stud books list the lineage of all animals bred within a facility. Pedigree papers travel with an individual animal as a record of that animal's lineage. Both tools are essential to breeders to keep track of the breeding programs in operation.

There are several ways to decide which animals should be bred, and some or all of them weigh into the decisions that the animal breeders make. The physical appearance and the health of the animal usually come first; this is called mass selection—where the animal is selected of its own merits. If the animal has successfully reproduced before, this is called progeny selection. The animal can be bred again, knowing that the animal has produced desirable offspring previously. However, if that particular animal becomes genetically overrepresented in a generation, then the breeder runs the risk of inbreeding with the generations to follow. So the value of that animal's offspring has to be weighed against the need for diversity in parents. Family selection also determines the value of reproducing an animal. Some genetic diversity can come from breeding siblings of a good breeder, but it may not be enough diversity if the breeder is working with a limited stock of animals. Pedigree is the final determiner in evaluating a breeding animal.

Requirements

High School

High school students seeking to enter this field will find that the more agriculture and science courses they select in high school, the better prepared they will be. In addition, courses in mathematics, business, communications, chemistry, and mechanics are valuable.

Postsecondary Training

Nine months to two years at a technical school or a college diploma are the usual minimum credentials for animal breeders and technicians. Many colleges now offer two- and four-year programs in animal science or animal husbandry where additional knowledge, skills, and specialized training may be acquired. Besides learning the scientific side of animal breeding, including instruction in genetics, animal physiology, and some veterinary science, students also take business classes that help them see the field from an economic point of view. With the increasing use of technology for breeding livestock and domesticated nonfarm animals, a bachelor's degree becomes more important for succeeding in the field. Master's and doctoral degrees are useful for the most specialized fields and the careers that require the most sophisticated genetic planning. Higher degrees are required for potential teachers in the field, and the current work being done in cloning is done exclusively by people with doctorates.

Whether trained by experience, at an academic institution, or both, all new hires at major breeding companies are usually put through some type of training program.

Certification or Licensing

Certification is not required but nearly all major companies have certification programs which can enhance earnings and opportunities.

Exploring

Organizations such as the 4-H Club and the National FFA Organization (formerly Future Farmers of America) offer good opportunities for hearing about, visiting, and participating in farm activities. Programs sponsored by 4-H allow students to learn firsthand about breeding small animals for show. Other organizations, such as the American Kennel Club, sponsor clubs dedicated to particular breeds, and these clubs usually provide educational programs on raising and breeding these animals.

Other opportunities might include volunteering at a breeding farm or ranch, kennel, or stable where animals are bred and sold. This will give you a chance to see the work required, and begin to get experience in practical skills for the job.

For at-home experience, raising pets is a good introduction to the skills needed in basic animal maintenance. Learning how to care for, feed, and house a pet provides some basic knowledge of working with animals. In addition, interested students can learn more about this field by reading books on animals and their care. But unless you have background and experience in breeding, and a good mentor to work with, it is not recommended that you start breeding your pet. There are literally millions of unwanted dogs and cats that come from mixed breeds or unpedigreed purebreds, and many of these animals are destroyed because there are no homes for them.

Other opportunities that provide animal maintenance experience include volunteering to work at animal shelters, veterinary offices, and pet breeders' businesses.

Employers

Animal breeders and technicians used to work for themselves, but today most are employed by corporate breeders. A few may still own their own livestock ranches, and some do it only as a sideline or hobby.

Starting Out

Many junior colleges participate in "learn-and-earn" programs, in which the college and prospective employer jointly provide the student's training, both in the classroom and through on-the-job work with livestock and other animals. Most technical programs offer placement services for graduates, and the demand for qualified people often exceeds the supply.

Advancement

Even when a good training or technical program is completed, the graduate often must begin work at a low level before advancing to positions with more responsibility. But the technical program graduate will advance much more rapidly to positions of major responsibility and greater financial reward than the untrained worker.

Those graduates willing to work hard and keep abreast of changes in their field may advance to *livestock breeder, feedlot manager, supervisor,* or *artificial breeding distributor*. If they have the necessary capital, they can own their own livestock ranches.

Earnings

Salaries vary widely depending on employer, the technicians' educational and agricultural background, the kind of animal the technicians work with, and the geographical areas in which they work. In general, the salaries of all agricultural technicians tend to be lower in the northeastern part of the nation and higher in California and some parts of the Midwest, such as Minnesota and Iowa. According to the National Association of Colleges and Employers, starting salaries for animal breeders with a bachelor's degree averaged $27,600 in 1999. Salaries for technicians are significantly lower, ranging from approximately $15,000 to $26,000 a year or more. In addition, many technicians receive food and housing benefits that can amount to several thousand dollars a year. Other fringe benefits vary according to employer but can include paid vacation time, health insurance, and pension benefits.

Work Environment

Working conditions vary from operation to operation, but certain factors always exist. Much of the work is done inside in all types of facilities. Barns, pens, and stables are the most common facilities for farm animals; nonfarm animals may be bred in private homes or housing facilities. Both types of work often require long, irregular hours, and work on Sundays and holidays. Salaries are usually commensurate with the hours worked, and there are usually slack seasons when time off is given to compensate any extra hours worked. But for people with a strong desire to work with animals, long working hours or other less desirable conditions are offset by the benefits of this career.

Animal breeders and technicians are often their own bosses and make their own decisions. While this can be an asset to those who value independence, prospective animal breeders and technicians must realize that self-discipline is the most valuable trait for success.

Outlook

Continuing changes are expected in the next few years, in both the production and the marketing phases of the animal production industry. Because of the costs involved, it is almost impossible for a one-person operation to stay in business for farm animals. As a result, cooperatives of consultants and corporations will become more prevalent with greater emphasis placed on specialization. This, in turn, will increase the demand for technical program graduates. Other factors, such as small profit margins, the demand for more uniform products, and an increasing foreign market, will result in a need for more specially trained personnel. This is a new era of specialization in the animal production industry; graduates of animal production technology programs have an interesting and rewarding future ahead of them.

For domesticated nonfarm animals, breeders usually work with individual species and do so because they love the animals, not for a profit-bearing business. According to the American Kennel Club, the average dog breeder loses money on each successful litter.

For More Information

For information on careers, education, and financial aid opportunities, contact:

American Society of Animal Science
1111 North Dunlap Avenue
Savoy, IL 61874
Tel: 217-356-3182
Email: asas@assochq.org
Web: http://www.asas.org/

The following is a central agency for national public information distribution and acts as the industry liaison for the beef cattle business. For more information, contact its national headquarters.

National Cattlemen's Association
PO Box 3469
Englewood, CO 80155
Tel: 303-694-0305

The AKC is the national authority on dog breeding and pedigrees.

American Kennel Club (AKC)
51 Madison Avenue
New York, NY 10010
Web: http://www.akc.org/akc

For more information on education and opportunities in the agricultural field, contact:

4-H
Stop 2225
1400 Independence Avenue, SW
Washington, DC 20250-2225
Tel: 202-720-2908
Web: http://www.4h-usa.org

National FFA Organization
6060 FFA Drive
PO Box 68960
Indianapolis, IN 46268
Tel: 317-802-6060
Web: http://www.ffa.org

Aquaculturists

School Subjects

Biology
Business

Personal Skills

Mechanical/manipulative
Technical/scientific

Work Environment

Indoors and outdoors
Primarily one location

Minimum Education Level

Bachelor's degree

Salary Range

$16,640 to $26,416 to $52,400

Certification or Licensing

Required by certain states

Outlook

Faster than the average

Overview

Aquaculturists, also known as *fish farmers, fish culturists*, or *mariculturists*, raise fish, shellfish, or other aquatic life (such as aquatic plants) under controlled conditions for profit and human consumption.

History

The roots of fish farming go far back in history. Fish culturing began in at least 1000 BC, possibly even earlier in Egypt and China. Ancient China introduced ornamental-goldfish breeding to Japan, which in turn developed ornamental-carp breeding. Ancient Romans were the first mariculturists, creating ponds for fish breeding that let in ocean water. Brackish-water fish farms existed in Java by about 1400 AD. However, historically, the vast majority of food-fish has come from capture, not farming. Capture fishery worldwide grew at rates of about 4 percent per year through most of the 20th century, but increased by only 0.6 percent between 1986 and 1987 (to about 93 million metric tons). Since then, growth rates of less than 1 percent per year have been the norm. In a nutshell, the natural supply of fish is shrinking—natural waters are being "fished out"—while fish consumption is rising. Enter aquaculture.

U.S. aquaculture began in the 1920s and 1930s with some farming of minnows for bait and with growth of catfish, bass, and other food-fish farming in the 1950s, largely in the South. In 1975, U.S. aquaculture produced 130 million pounds of fish; by 1987, it produced more than 400 million pounds. Today, U.S. aquaculture produces catfish, crawfish, salmon, trout, oysters, and other products. U.S. restaurants offer a wide range of fish produced by aquaculture, including salmon, shrimp, catfish, crabs, clams, mussels, lobster, carp, sturgeon, cod, and mahi-mahi (dolphin). As capture yields have leveled off, aquaculture yields have grown at rates of 7 percent per year or more. Today, aquaculture is nearly a $1 billion industry in the United States.

Some hope aquaculture can help meet food needs in developing countries. Fish is a healthier source of protein than meat and requires less energy to produce (about two pounds of feed for one pound of catfish, versus eight pounds of feed for one pound of beef). Aquaculture can still be done simply and cheaply, such as in a pond, using farm waste as fertilizer. (Such setups, however, produce less desirable fish, like carp.)

The Job

The term "aquaculturist" typically is used to describe someone who raises fish for profit. This is not a conservation job. Aquaculturists may have a degree in fish biology or other fish science, just like some of the people working for the U.S. Fish and Wildlife Service, National Biological Service, or other federal agencies, or for federal or state fish hatcheries. But they don't share those agencies' goal of protecting rare and endangered species.

Technically speaking, aquaculture can be done in fresh water, brackish (salty or somewhat salty) water, seawater, flooded fields, rice paddies, and other waters. Practically speaking, limited areas in the United States are appropriate for aquaculture. Right now, U.S. aquaculture is focused in the South (catfish), the West (salmon), and a few other areas (like bait farms in Arkansas). There must be markets for the products, capital to develop the site, appropriate water supplies, and proper structures for handling effluent. Conditions must be right; for example, catfish production in the South is successful because of the warmer waters, longer growing season, and other factors. Fish farms range in size from a few acres to 50 acres or more and typically focus on one type of fish (such as trout or catfish) or shellfish (such as clams, shrimp, or oysters). Rearing may be done in earth ponds, concrete ponds, or pens in seas, lakes, or ocean waters.

Fish farming differs significantly from regular farming. Fish are more complicated because of their environment—water. Also, intensely confined animals tend to be more susceptible to disease; many of these fish are in a confined space. Raising fish is more like a feedlot raising penned animals than a rancher raising cattle in open range lands. The raising of fish also requires closer monitoring than raising farm animals.

A primary goal of aquaculture is to increase fish production beyond what's possible in nature. In recent years, there's been a lot of research to determine which fish are most suited to fish farming, what to feed them and in what quantities, what conditions will optimize production and quality, and other areas. Biologists and other research scientists have experimented with things like cross-breeding for better genetics (such as for increased egg production). Commercial feeds and supplements have been developed to boost fish size. Aquaculturists also have been working on least-cost feeding formulas, or ratios of lowest-costing food to highest quantity and quality fish, for better profits. Experiments with the effects of light on growth, with limiting feeding, and other research studies also have been conducted. Since confined fish may be more susceptible to diseases, researchers also have developed drugs such as fluoroquinolone for approval by the Food and Drug Administration.

In fish farming, eggs are stripped from the female fish, fertilized by milt from the male fish, and placed in moist pans or hatchery trays. These are put in incubators to spawn the eggs. Resulting fingerlings are put in the rearing ponds or other waters for further growth. They may be fed high-protein food or cereal with vitamins or minerals so they will achieve good size and quality. Aquaculturists also might monitor water quality, add drugs to fight disease, and otherwise optimize growing conditions. Once the right size is reached, which can take up to three years or more, the fish are removed from the water, counted, weighed, and loaded into a truck or dressed and packed in ice for shipment to the buyer.

In shellfish farming, clams, oysters, and other shellfish are cultivated in specially prepared beds near the shoreline and then harvested. Tide flats are laid out and dikes created to control water drainage at low tide. The spawn of oysters or other shellfish, known as spat, are sown in the beds and may be covered with sand or broken shells. When the tide is up and the beds are covered with water, the beds may be dragged with nets to remove crabs, starfish, or other predators. Workers also might pour oil around the beds to discourage predators from getting the crop. At low tide, workers walk into the bed and collect full-grown shellfish for packing and sale.

Positions within the fish farm operation may include a manager or superintendent, supervisors, and workers. A manager or superintendent heads the operation, helping to establish policies and procedures and conferring with biologists or other scientists on optimal feeding and other conditions. They also may handle hiring, firing, payroll, and other personnel matters; monitor budgets and costs; and do other administrative work. Supervisors oversee the spawning, rearing, harvesting, and other day-to-day farming activities. They might train workers, prepare reports, and help monitor quality control. Workers may be called assistants, attendants, bed workers, or similar titles, and they do the labor-intensive parts of the fish farming operation.

Scientists working within the fish farming operation, or in research facilities supporting aquaculture, include *fisheries biologists* and *harvest management biologists*. They focus on fish living habits, relationships, growth, rearing, stocking, and the like.

Some aquaculturists work in universities trying to find ways to improve aquaculture production. For example, experiments done at Auburn University's aquaculture center have shown that limiting feed actually can increase fish weight and protein amount. Since aquaculture is still not that well developed in the United States, researchers and economists also have developed feasibility studies, focusing on the potential viability of different types of aquaculture for various regions. For example, a 1994 University of Florida study said tropical fish, aquatic plants, and bait-fish might be the future of aquaculture in that state, rather than catfish farming. Research goes on worldwide; for example, in 1995 the Institute of Aquaculture in Scotland was studying the use of immune system stimulants to encourage macrophage growth in fish.

Requirements

High School

Most jobs in aquaculture require a bachelor's degree, so follow a college preparatory plan of English, history, government, foreign language, and other courses recommended by your guidance counselor. Take science courses, particularly biology courses, to prepare for a marine science, aquaculture, or biology college program. Some management experience is also important, so take courses in business and accounting.

Postsecondary Training

A bachelor's degree is the minimum requirement for jobs in aquaculture beyond the laborer or assistant level. Researchers usually have an advanced degree in their specialty. Jobs in aquaculture tend to be more plentiful than jobs with fish and wildlife management agencies (which are very tough to get), but the educational requirements are basically the same. Without a bachelor's degree, it is very difficult to find work at the professional level. In part, fish farming is more complicated today, given new understanding of ecology (such as how one organism impacts another), fish genetics (such as how fish adapt themselves genetically to a natural environment), and other areas. A bachelor's degree in fish and wildlife biology is the primary path into this field. A minor in business or accounting may also be valuable to a prospective aquaculturist.

Certification or Licensing

The American Fisheries Society certifies associate fishery scientists, fishery scientists, fish pathologists (specialists in fish disease), and fish health specialists. A certain number of hours of experience plus a written test are necessary. Both private and government fish people obtain these certifications. In some areas, they are required for obtaining some positions and for receiving raises and promotions.

Other Requirements

You should be people-oriented because you'll often work with private market suppliers, the public, and politicians. Good writing skills will come in handy in some positions, as will business and administrative skills like budgeting. A knowledge of computer modeling and statistics can help in newer areas like harvest management and population dynamics.

Exploring

Contact the American Fisheries Society for information about careers in aquaculture. Also, read *Aquaculture Magazine* and visit its Web site (http://www.aquaculturemag.com) to learn more about the issues of the industry. Any hands-on experience you can get, even in high school, will be helpful in landing a job. Through a "shadowing" project, you may be able to spend some time in a local hatchery at the side of an aquaculturist. Volunteering at one of the approximately 75 federal fish hatcheries nationwide, or a state hatchery, is an option. Contact local hatcheries, go meet the people there, and find out about applying for a job. Experience at a pet shop that sells different varieties of salt-water fish, or at a state aquarium, can also give you insight into the industry.

Employers

Aquaculturists can find work with commercial and private fish farms owned by corporations, states, or individuals. They may work with a small family-run operation or with a large operation employing hundreds of people. According to a recent survey by the U.S. Department of Agriculture (USDA), the top five producing states by value are Mississippi, Arkansas, Florida, Maine, and Alabama. The USDA also reports that 68 percent of the fish farms are located in the southern United States. Facilities, however, range across the country and include rainbow trout farms in Idaho, oyster farms in Washington state, and salmon farms in Maine. Some universities also hire aquaculturists, as does the U.S. Fish and Wildlife Service, and other national organizations.

Starting Out

Aquaculture work usually is easier to find than fishery or wildlife agency work, but it can't hurt to follow some of the same strategies used to land those jobs: namely, get experience. Become a student chapter member of the American Fisheries Society and explore this group's national job listings. Work with your university's placement department. A person looking for a job needs to be pretty flexible. Since U.S. aquaculture is more developed in some areas, such as the South and West, your first job may take you to a new region.

International opportunities are possible, too. Those who have considered the Peace Corps should know that some volunteers work in aquaculture. (Peace Corps volunteers are U.S. citizens, over 18 years old, with a college education or at least three years' experience in their specialty.) Groups like UNICEF and USAID in Africa also use fish and wildlife specialists.

Beyond these types of organizations, other international job opportunities may be possible wherever aquaculture is practiced. Scandinavians raise a lot of coldwater fish; the Japanese raise shellfish, algae, and kelp. Of course, pollution has made some fresh waters in Europe, like the Thames in England, unsuitable for fish farming activities.

Advancement

In fish farming, the professional typically enters as a *fish biologist* or other fish scientist and advances to some kind of manager or supervisor position. As noted earlier, state certification may help speed this process in some areas. Fish farming is a business; each operation is different, but further raises or promotions are likely to hinge on profits, customer satisfaction, development and sustaining of new markets, and similar business successes. On the research side, advancement will depend on the individual employer. With a young U.S. aquaculture industry clamoring for information, new research and development, and improved aquaculture technologies, it's possible for fish scientists in research to have a big impact with their studies and reap the financial benefits of doing so.

Earnings

Earnings in aquaculture can vary greatly. Aquaculture farms employ graduate students in assistantships, as well as experienced professionals with Ph.D.s in genetics. Entry level technicians may begin at $8 an hour; those with a great deal of experience and a degree may begin at a salary of $28,000 a year. According to the 1998 edition of the *O*Net Dictionary of Occupational Titles*, the mean annual earnings for all workers in aquaculture was $26,416. The National Association of Colleges and Employers estimates that biologists with bachelor's degrees, working in private industry in 1997, had a starting wage of $25,000 a year; those with master's degrees earned $26,900; and those with doctorates started at $52,400.

Work Environment

A fish farm is not much different from a mink farm or other operation aimed at raising high volumes of animals. Those who don't like that idea should think twice about this career. On the other hand, fish farms and fish hatcheries give aquaculturists the opportunity to work outdoors, to apply scientific education in a concrete way, and to make a difference in a young and growing industry. Some fish farm operations are small and some are large; trout farming, for example, is made up of both small and large operations. This variety allows workers in the field to find the size and style of operation that's right for them.

Fishery and wildlife careers sound romantic, and in some ways, they are; that's why they're so popular. Much of the work of an aquaculturist, however, is very pragmatic: fighting fish diseases, for example.

People drawn to fishery and wildlife management tend to like the outdoors. Keep in mind, however, that this work also involves frequent interaction with others and the successful aquaculturist should have good people skills. Those who work in administrative positions are mainly business people and don't work directly with the fish.

Outlook

The outlook for U.S. aquaculture is promising. A subcommittee of the U.S. Department of Commerce is predicting there will be a 70 percent increase in world seafood demand by 2025. Commercial fisheries are over harvested, so much of this demand will be met by aquaculture. Aquaculture's ability to meet this demand, however, will depend on the growth and development of the industry. Many universities are currently benefiting from grants which allow them to explore better methods of growing and harvesting product, and preventing disease. Advances in these areas will help to lower risk and increase profits, attracting more interest in the industry.

The business is regulated, but on the whole the government seems interested in helping to support and develop the industry. Federal assistance with development of needed aquaculture drugs and chemicals is one sign of this.

For More Information

For information about certification and the professional society serving fisheries scientists, contact:

American Fisheries Society
5410 Grosvenor Lane, Suite 110
Bethesda, MD 20814-2199
Tel: 301-897-8616
Web: http://www.fisheries.org

For information about industry journals, publications, membership, and job postings, contact:

World Aquaculture Society (U.S. Branch)
143 J.M. Parker Coliseum
Louisiana State University
Baton Rouge, LA 70803
Tel: 225-388-3137
Web: http://www.was.org

This Web site provides information and links to state, national, and international associations, publications, and job services involved with aquaculture.

Aquaculture Network Information Center
Web: http://aquanic.org

Beekeepers

School Subjects

Agriculture
Biology
Earth science

Personal Skills

Mechanical/manipulative
Technical/scientific

Work Environment

Primarily outdoors
One location with some travel

Minimum Education Level

Apprenticeship

Salary Range

$10,808 to $13,339 to $20,781

Certification or Licensing

Voluntary (certification)
Required by certain states (licensing)

Outlook

Decline

Overview

Beekeepers, also known as *apiarists*, care for and raise honeybees for commercial and agricultural purposes, such as honey production and crop pollination. Their duties might include assembling beehives and other equipment, buying and selling bees, establishing settlements close to pollination-dependent crops, transporting wild beehives to a central location, raising queen bees, and harvesting and selling honey. Beekeepers may work on farms or small plots of land to raise bees to assist in the production of grain and other agricultural crops. Beekeeping may be a full-time job, a "sideline" job, or a hobby. Beekeepers usually work alone or as a member of a small team.

History

Early rock paintings in Spain and Africa depict people gathering honey from trees or rock crevices while bees flew around them. Ancient Egyptian relics show the beekeeper taking honey from a hive while a helper drives the bees away with smoke. There is evidence that the Mayans kept a stingless, honey-storing bee. Relics from Belize and Mexico, including stone disks thought to have been the end stoppers on wooden log-shaped hives, represent the oldest artifacts related to beekeeping in the New World.

Early honey gatherers probably accidentally discovered that smoke calms bees when they used fire to drive off other animals. Beekeeping may have originally developed following the observation that swarms of bees will settle in any container with a dark, protected interior space. Pottery and natural containers, such as holes in trees or logs, provide shelter and protection for hive establishment. In some forested areas of Europe, hive clusters made from logs can still be found. Horizontal pottery hives are used along the Mediterranean, and straw hives, known as "skeps," are still used in Belgium and France.

The honeybee, which is not native to North America, was shipped to the colonies from England in the first half of the 17th century. For many years, straw skeps were used for hives, followed by log "gums." With these crude hives, it was difficult to know when the bees had problems with disease or starvation or if they were queenless; the beekeeper could not inspect the combs to determine what was wrong. By the same token, it was difficult to extract honey from these hives without damaging or destroying the bee colony. Typically, beekeepers had to kill their swarms each fall by burning sulphur at the entrance of the hive; then the honey and beeswax could be removed.

In the 17th and 18th centuries, beekeepers began to build movable-comb hives, which enabled them to inspect combs without damaging them. In 1789, Francis Huber invented the first movable-frame hive. The combs in this hive could be easily inspected like the pages of a book. In 1852, Lorenzo Langstroth, a minister from Pennsylvania, patented a hive with movable frames that hung from the top of the hive, leaving a 3/8-inch space between the frames and the hive body (the exact spacing at which bees will build comb they can move around, referred to today as "beespace"). By the turn of the 20th century, most beekeepers were using Langstroth's system. Langstroth is known as "the father of modern beekeeping."

Modern beekeeping methods evolved very rapidly following the invention of Langstroth's system. Wax-comb foundation, which made possible the consistent production of high-quality combs of worker cells, was invented in 1857. The centrifugal honey extractor was invented in 1865, enabling large-scale production of honey, and later in the century the radial extractor (where both sides of the frame are extracted at the same time) was invented. In 1889, G. M. Doolittle of New York developed the system for rearing queen bees that is still used today by all commercial queen-rearers. Bee smokers and veils evolved and improved. Also around this time, leaders in American beekeeping learned of the merits of the Italian honeybee, and they began to import these bees into the states. Today, the American version of the Italian honeybee is still widely used throughout the country.

Today the most significant advances in beekeeping are related to the areas of bee management and the extracting process. In general, the dimensions of hives and frames have become more standardized; drugs are available for disease control; artificial insemination of queen bees is being used commercially; and colony rental is being used increasingly for crop pollination.

The Job

In the spring, beekeepers set up new hives and repair old ones. A beginning beekeeper will have to purchase bees from a dealer. The beekeeper will set up the hive near an orchard or field where nectar will be available for the bees.

A beekeeper's primary task is the care and feeding of the bees. The hives must be inspected regularly for mite infestations and diseases. The bees must also occasionally be fed, especially during the winter months when forage is unavailable.

Beekeepers ensure that the bees and their surroundings are healthy and clean. They watch out for robber bees, who will try to rob food from other hives when they are unable to find enough nectar to make honey. Beekeepers make it easier for the bees to defend the hive by limiting the size of the entrance. Beekeepers must also watch for "swarming," a situation in which about half of the bees from a colony look for a new place to live because the hive has become too crowded or is no longer adequately ventilated. To prevent swarming, the entrance to the hive can be enlarged to improve air circulation, especially during the summer. The beekeeper might also clip the queen's wing to prevent her from leaving with the swarm or move half the bees to a new hive with another queen.

The queen bee also requires special attention. In a properly functioning hive the queen will be almost constantly laying eggs. If she becomes sick or old, the beekeeper will need to replace her.

Beekeepers must wear special equipment when working with bees. A veil and plastic helmet protect the beekeeper's head and neck from the stings of angry bees. Some beekeepers also wear thick clothing and gloves for protection, although many professionals feel that the thick clothes are too bulky and hot. Their choice is to risk the occasional sting to gain the benefit of wearing lighter clothing.

A beekeeper uses smoke to keep the bees from swarming in anger. An angry bee gives off a scent that alarms the rest of the hive. Smoke, produced in a special smoker device, masks the alarm scent, preventing the formation of an attack swarm.

Beekeepers must purchase or construct special enclosures to contain the beehives. The most popular model in the United States is the "Langstroth" hive, a rectangular wood and metal construction that sits upon a stand to keep it dry.

Harvesting honey is an important part of the beekeeper's job. When the honey is ready for harvesting, beekeepers seal the honeycomb with beeswax. They remove the frames of honeycombs and take them to the extractor, where the honey is spun out of the honeycomb. It is filtered and drained into a tank. The honey is stored in five-gallon buckets or in fifty-five gallon drums. This is a part of beekeeping where physical strength is important.

Beekeepers also spend time keeping data on their colonies. Their records track information regarding the queens, any extra food that may have been required, honey yields and dates, and so forth.

Requirements

High School

If you're interested in beekeeping, you should take high school classes in business and mathematics to prepare you for the records-keeping aspect of this work. Science classes, such as natural sciences, biology, and earth science, will give you an understanding of the environment as well as processes such as pollination. If your high school offers agriculture classes, be sure to take those for added understanding of crop and animal production. Wood shop classes will also be useful if you intend to build your own hives.

Postsecondary Training

While no formal postsecondary training is required for this work, the U.S. Department of Labor's Bureau of Apprenticeship and Training offers an apprenticeship program in beekeeping. Their Beekeeper Apprenticeship Program is an 8,000-hour program that involves both on-the-job training in beekeeping skills and related technical instruction. This program may be sponsored by employers, employer associations, or joint employer/union partnerships. Currently 27 states administer these apprenticeships through their own administrative council. For information about all beekeeping apprenticeship programs, contact the U.S. Department of Labor.

Certification or Licensing

Beekeepers who complete the government-sanctioned apprenticeship program may apply for a Certificate of Completion from the U.S. Department of Labor.

Beekeeping licenses are issued at the state level, and requirements vary from state to state. Some states do not require a license at all, although almost every state requires that the commercial beekeeper register every hive.

Other Requirements

While a love of nature and the ability and desire to work alone were once among the most important characteristics for a beekeeper, many beekeepers today feel that a shrewd business sense and marketing savvy are what's most necessary to survive. Most commercial beekeepers seem to agree that the key to success as a beekeeper lies less in working with the bees than in working in the commercial business marketplace. Therefore, a good understanding of economics and basic business accounting is essential to the practice of beekeeping.

Nevertheless, beekeepers still need physical strength, endurance, and a love of the outdoors to be successful. Of course, a beekeeper will also be working with large groups of insects, so this is not a job for people with aversions to insects or allergies to bee venom.

Exploring

If you are interested in beekeeping, you should contact a local beekeeping association for advice and guidance. You should find an experienced, successful beekeeper who is willing to share his or her knowledge. A part-time job with a beekeeper would be an ideal introduction to the trade, but the opportunity simply to observe a beekeeper and ask questions is also invaluable. Read as much as you can about beekeeping. Start by checking out your local library for books on the subject; look for books written specifically for your part of the country. You should also subscribe to a beekeeping magazine, such as *BeeCulture* or *American Bee Journal*. Join a local chapter of 4-H or the National FFA (formerly Future Farmers of America). While you may not gain direct experience with beekeeping, you will be able to work on agricultural or other projects and gain management experience.

Employers

Beekeeping is a small and specialized profession. Some in the field estimate that there are currently under 2,000 professional beekeepers in the United States. The vast majority of beekeepers today do not depend on beekeeping for their income; they're known in the trade as "sideliners" or hobbyists. Most beekeepers run their own independent business rather than work for a large commercial establishment.

Starting Out

Since most beekeepers work independently, the most likely route of entry is to learn the basics and invest in some starting equipment. You can contact your local beekeeping association for advice. Keep in mind that if you hope to raise bees for commercial profit, you will need a substantial amount of capital to get started, and you're likely to face several years without profits while you work to increase honey production. If you live in an area where bees are raised, you should contact local beekeepers who may hire you for part-time or seasonal work.

Advancement

Advancement in this field most often comes as beekeepers increase the number of hives they own and increase their commercial sales. It isn't likely that new beekeepers will be able to support themselves by beekeeping alone; most likely it will be a hobby or a sideline to supplement their living.

Earnings

In 1997, the Economic Research Institute estimated yearly earnings for beekeepers with one year of experience at $10,808; for beekeepers with five years of experience at $13,339; and for beekeepers with 10 years of experience at $20,781. However, based on the market value of honey and the cost of production—especially among medium to small operations—it is often difficult to turn a profit. Some beekeepers are able to earn income through raising hives to rent to crop growers. Rental fees vary, but it's not unusual for a beekeeper to get $40 to $50 per hive for a two- to three-week period. Some small-scale beekeepers are able to market and sell specialty items (for example, beeswax-based products) that can be profitable, but again, this is usually a hobby or sideline, not an exclusive source of income.

Work Environment

Beekeepers work primarily outdoors. The "in-season" hours (mostly in the spring and summer) can be very long, and the work can be physically challenging. Those who enjoy nature might well be suited for beekeeping, but there are indoor components to the work as well, such as tending to business records, processing honey, and caring for equipment. This is a field that requires discipline and the ability to work without supervision. A beekeeper must spend many hours working alone in tasks that can be grueling. Many beekeepers work part-time at the trade while performing other agricultural duties. Those with a sensitivity to bee stings should certainly avoid this industry, as—despite protective gear—stings are an inevitable part of the job.

Outlook

Since the 1980s, 90 percent of the nation's wild honeybees have been wiped out by tracheal and varroa mites. Many beekeepers find that their bee colonies dwindle by over half each year, while costs are up as much as 100 percent. With less than 2,000 commercial beekeepers currently in operation in the United States, and one third of our food supply dependent on honeybees for pollination, it might seem logical to assume that there will be increasing demand for their services in the future. However, since the North American Free Trade Agreement was passed, the need for orchard pollination services has shifted from the United States to Mexico. In addition, it is increasingly difficult for domestic producers to compete with the prices of imported honey. Foreign honey producers have fewer environmental regulations to abide by, lower wage rates to pay, and fewer worker benefits to provide. Thus, they are able to charge less for their product. Due to all of these factors, beekeepers in the United States are seeing demand for their services in decline.

For More Information

The American Beekeeping Federation acts on behalf of the beekeeping industry on issues affecting the interests and the economic viability of the various sectors of the industry. The organization sponsors an essay contest in conjunction with 4-H and also has a Honey Queen and Honey Princess Program. For more information, contact:

American Beekeeping Federation
PO Box 1038
Jesup, GA 31598-1038
Tel: 912-427-4233
Email: info@abfnet.org
Web: http://www.abfnet.org

For information about these organizations, contact:

4-H
Stop 2225
1400 Independence Avenue, SW
Washington, DC 20250-2225
Tel: 202-720-2908
Web: http://www.4h-usa.org

National FFA Organization
6060 FFA Drive
PO Box 68960
Indianapolis, IN 46268
Tel: 317-802-6060
Web: http://www.ffa.org

The National Honey Board serves the honey industry by increasing demand for honey and honey products. Check out the Web site for information on the industry.

National Honey Board
390 Lashley Street
Longmont, CO 80501-1421
Tel: 303-776-2337
Web: http://www.nhb.org

For more information on apprenticeship programs, contact:

U.S. Department of Labor
Bureau of Apprenticeship and Training
200 Constitution Avenue, NW
Washington, DC 20210
Tel: 202-219-5921
Web: http://www.doleta.gov/individ/apprent.asp

These magazines have information on the industry.

American Bee Journal
51 South 2nd Street
Hamilton, IL 62341
Tel: 217-847-3324
Web: http://www.dadant.com/abj.htm

BeeCulture
Tel: 800-289-7668, ext. 3255
Web: http://bee.airoot.com/beeculture

The Back Yard Beekeepers Association is a national club that provides their membership with interesting and practical information about the "how-to's" of beekeeping. The club also provides the general public with educational programs about honeybees and the benefits of beekeeping in the community. Use the Web site to locate a club near you.

Back Yard Beekeepers Association
Tel: 914-693-7312
Web: www.backyardbeekeepers.com

Canning and Preserving Industry Workers

School Subjects
Agriculture
Chemistry

Personal Skills
Following instructions
Technical/scientific

Work Environment
Primarily indoors
Primarily one location

Minimum Education Level
High school diploma

Salary Range
$10,000 to $21,300 to $30,500

Certification or Licensing
Required in certain positions

Outlook
Decline

Overview

Canning and preserving industry workers monitor equipment and perform routine tasks in food-processing plants that can, preserve, and quick-freeze such foods as vegetables, fruits, frozen dinners, jams, jellies, preserves, pickles, and soups. They also process and preserve seafood, including shrimp, oysters, crabs, clams, and fish.

History

As soon as people learned to grow and harvest food, they faced the problem of keeping that food from spoiling so that it could last until the next harvest. Centuries ago, people discovered that salting, drying, and pickling could preserve many meats, fruits, and vegetables. In colonial America, most of this preserving was done in the home. Families grew their own fruits and vegetables and preserved them to make them last through the winter months.

In 1795, the French government sought better ways to feed its army, especially ways to keep foods from spoiling, and offered a prize to anyone who could develop a method of keeping foods edible and portable for a long period of time. Nicolas Appert, a chef in Paris, took up the challenge and developed the first canning process. In 1810, Appert developed a system of bottling foods, corking the bottles and holding the corks in place with wire, and then heating the bottles. At the same time in England, the first tin-coated metal cans were developed, and these were soon applied to food preservation using Appert's method. Appert's process became known as canning.

Since the Industrial Revolution, and especially in the 20th century, advances in refrigeration and sanitation and new applications of many industrial processes of food preparation have almost completely transferred the business of preserving food to large factories. Freezing was applied to food preservation in the 1920s, and ways were sought to freeze foods as quickly as possible, thereby preserving not only their flavor but also their nutritional value. Scientists also discovered that certain chemicals could preserve food by killing off microorganisms or preventing them from reproducing. Later, irradiation became another controversial method of food preservation.

Very few Americans today grow and preserve large quantities of their own food, and factory-preserved fruits, fish, soup, and vegetables are found in almost every refrigerator and kitchen cupboard in the nation. Canning and preservation techniques have made it possible for people to enjoy foods from all over the world, and at all times of the year.

For much of the past century, canning and preserving were labor-intensive; that is, they required many people to manually perform the various steps of processing, preserving, and packaging foods. In recent years, automated machinery and equipment, which are often computer-controlled, have greatly increased the quantity of foods that can be processed and have made it possible for many foods to be processed, canned, and preserved without ever being touched by human hands.

The Job

In order to operate successfully, a food-processing plant must have plenty of the foodstuff it processes. Therefore, many workers in the canning and preserving industry work outside processing plants arranging for this supply of raw materials. *Field contractors* negotiate with farmers to grow certain kinds of food crops for processing. They work with farmers to decide what to plant, how to grow the crop, and when to harvest it. They reach agreements concerning price, the quantity that will be delivered, and the quality standards that the crop must meet. *Purchasing agents* purchase raw materials and other goods for processing.

When unprocessed food arrives at the factory, *graders*, including fruit-buying graders, examine produce and record its quality, or grade, and mark it for separation by class, size, color, and condition.

Wharf laborers unload catches of fish for processing from the wharf and transport the fish to the processing plant's storage area. *Fish-bin tenders* sort fish according to species and size.

At the plant, the *plant superintendent* coordinates processing activities to coincide with crop harvesting. The *plant manager* hires workers, contacts buyers, and coordinates maintenance and operation of plant machinery.

Most processing of food is done with automatic machines. *Dumping-machine operators* run machines that grip, tilt, and dump boxes of produce onto conveyor belts leading to washing vats. Workers then wash food and inspect the produce, removing damaged or spoiled items before they can be processed. *Sieve-grader tenders* and *sorting-machine operators* tend machines that sort vegetables, shrimp, and pickles according to size.

Many foods are bathed in brine, a concentrated solution of salt in water that acts as a preservative. *Brine makers* measure ingredients for the solution and boil it in a steam cooker for a specified amount of time. They test the solution's salinity with a hydrometer and pump it to a processing vat. They may also operate the vats and empty and clean them when necessary.

Plants that process fish and shellfish may kill, shell, and clean the fish before processing. *Crab butchers* butcher live crabs before canning. *Fish cleaners* and *fish-cleaning-machine operators* scale, slice open, and eviscerate fish. Using a shucking knife, *shellfish shuckers* pry open oyster, clam, and scallop shells and remove the meat. Shrimp are often shelled by machines that are operated by workers who must make adjustments according to the size of the shrimp. Later *separator operators* remove any sand or remaining shell particles from shellfish meats using water or air-agitating machines. Alternatively, *bone pickers* look for shell particles by placing shellfish meats under ultraviolet light and picking shell bits out by hand. Other workers operate machines that wash, steam, brine, and peel shellfish.

Often only one part of a fruit or vegetable is wanted for processing. Many workers operate machines that peel or extract the desired parts from produce. *Finisher operators* run machines that remove the skin and seeds from tomatoes, leaving pulp that is used in sauces and catsup. *Lye-peel operators* run machines that use lye and water to remove skins of fruits and vegetables. *Fruit-press operators* run power presses to extract juice from fruit for flavorings and syrup, and *extractor-machine operators* extract juice from citrus fruits.

Food must often be cut into pieces of the proper size and shape for preserving. *Meat blenders* grind meat for use in baby food. Many workers operate machines that cut or chop produce, and *fish butchers* and *fish choppers* cut fish into pieces and lengths for freezing or canning.

Next, foods are cooked. Some are cooked before and others after they are sealed in packages. Many vegetables are blanched (scalded with hot water or steam) before packaging, by *blanching-machine operators*. *Kettle cooks* and *kettle cook helpers* cook other fish, fruits, and vegetables in large kettles before packaging. These workers must measure and load water and uncooked food into the kettles; stir, monitor, and test foods as they cook; and remove cooked food from the kettles. Other workers cook fish, meat, and vegetables by deep-frying before freezing. *Vacuum-kettle cooks* prepare fruits and berries for jam and jelly.

Other foods, including many vegetables, are processed after they have been sealed in cans. *Packers* fill cans or jars with food to specified volume and weight. Other workers operate closing machines to put an airtight seal on the containers. Containers are then taken to retort chambers. Retorts are like huge steam pressure cookers, and they can heat food containers to temperatures between 240 degrees Fahrenheit and 260 degrees Fahrenheit. *Retort operators* load, start, and stop these machines according to specifications. Food must then be quickly cooled to stop cooking. Canning and preserving workers use pasteurizers to kill bacteria in bottles, canned foods, and beverages using a hot water spray or steam.

Some food is preserved using brine. *Picklers* mix ingredients for pickling vegetables, fruits, fish, and meat and soak these foods for a specified period of time. *Briners* immerse fresh fish fillets in brine to condition them for freezing.

Some food is prepared for canning by removing moisture, and some fish is smoked to preserve it. *Fish smokers* put salt-cured fish on racks in a smoke chamber and turn a valve to admit smoke into the chamber.

Many foods are frozen fresh or after blanching. *Freezing-room workers* move racks of packaged food in and out of freezing rooms. They keep track of the amount of time food has been in the freezing room and remove the food when it is sufficiently frozen to transport to a warehouse or onto delivery trucks. *Freezer-tunnel operators* quick-freeze foods.

Other foods, especially fruits, are preserved by drying. *Dehydrator tenders* bleach and dehydrate fruit, while other workers dry eggs, milk, and potatoes.

Once food has been canned, it is labeled, tested, and inspected. *Vacuum testers* tap can lids to make sure they are vacuum sealed. *Can inspectors* check seams of closed food and beverage cans by cutting and taking measurements of seams of sample cans. *X-ray inspectors* x-ray jars of baby food to ensure they contain no foreign materials.

Other workers clean cooking kettles and other equipment. *Production helpers* perform a variety of unskilled tasks in canning and preserving plants. Workers may also be designated according to the food they prepare: steak sauce makers, mincemeat makers, relish blenders, and horseradish makers, for example.

Cook room supervisors and *preparation supervisors* monitor and coordinate the activities of workers in preparing and canning foods. *Fish-processing supervisors* train new workers and inspect fish.

In large plants, each worker may perform one specific task. In smaller plants, one worker may perform many of the tasks necessary to preserve the food.

Requirements

High School

There are no minimum educational requirements for many food-processing jobs, although most employers prefer to hire high school graduates; a high school diploma is essential for those seeking advancement. Beginners seldom need previous experience, and usually they can learn their jobs quickly. Generally there is up to one month of on-the-job training.

Postsecondary Training

Many plants provide orientation sessions for new workers and programs on safety and sanitation. For those who aspire to management positions, a college degree is recommended, with studies in accounting, management, and other business courses as well as chemistry.

Certification or Licensing

Some skilled and technical staff in plants in some states must be licensed. Retort room supervisors are required by the Food and Drug Administration to attend an instructional program in retort operation.

Other Requirements

Manual dexterity is a useful characteristic for many workers in the canning and preserving industry, as are reliability and willingness to learn.

Exploring

Students may arrange to tour a food-processing plant in their area. Such a visit can be a good way to get a general overview of the jobs in the plant. Talking to people employed in different jobs in canning or preserving plants is another good way to learn something about the field. Because some food-processing work is seasonal, part-time job opportunities for students may be limited. However, temporary employment, such as during summer harvest season, may be possible.

Employers

Canning and preserving work is available in a variety of manufacturing plants. The type of products to be canned or preserved depends in part on what grows, grazes, or swims in a particular area. Coastal areas may have fish-processing plants, while the Midwest has more meat products. Farm regions may have plants that process products grown nearby. However, because of refrigeration and other technology, other factors, such as shipping routes and access to workers, may determine where plants are located. Manufacturers may be small companies or multinational organizations.

Starting Out

Applying to canneries, freezing plants, and other food-processing plants is the most direct method of finding work in this area. Employers may advertise openings in newspaper want ads or with the state employment service. Those interested in processing fish and seafood may find year-round work in canneries and processing ships in Alaska or follow the fishing seasons along the west and east coasts.

Advancement

Workers with a high school education start out as sorters or helpers or in similar unskilled positions. Advancement opportunities from these positions are limited. In time, some workers can move into field contractor positions. For those interested in more advanced positions, such as food technologists and food scientists, a college degree in a related course of study is required.

Earnings

Although some products can be processed at any time during the year, the level of activity in many food-processing plants varies with the season, and earnings of workers vary accordingly. Larger plants overcome the seasonality of their food products by maintaining large inventories of raw foodstuffs, and workers for these plants generally work full-time throughout the year. Earnings for workers in the canning and preserving industry vary widely. Many positions, especially at the entry level, pay little more than the minimum wage. The average earnings range from $19,000 to $21,000 per year; canned specialties workers earn an average of $30,500 per year.

Generally, seasonal workers earn an hourly wage; some, particularly those working on processing ships or for canneries in Alaska, also receive board and lodging. Benefits vary from company to company.

Work Environment

Canning and preserving plants are located in many parts of the country. Most plants are located close to the supply source and are staffed by local people who sometimes hold other jobs as well. During harvest season, plants may operate 24 hours a day, with three work shifts.

In plants where food is frozen, some workers spend considerable time in temperatures that are well below freezing. These workers wear special clothing and take periodic warm-up breaks during the day. Canneries, on the other hand, may be damp, noisy, and odorous. In some jobs, workers need to be on their feet for long periods, and often the tasks are very repetitive.

Outlook

In 1998, there were 50,000 workers employed in this industry. The use of automated equipment and computer technology throughout the food-processing industry means that fewer people will be needed to process, preserve, and can foods. However, wherever it is efficient and economical, machines will take over the tasks that people have been doing. Therefore a decline in the industry is projected through 2008. Researchers and technical workers with specialized expertise and college-level training will have the best employment opportunities.

In some kinds of food processing, such as the fish canneries in Alaska, employment levels are related to weather and other natural factors that vary from year to year.

For More Information

For news and statistics on the frozen food industry, contact:

American Frozen Food Institute
2000 Corporate Ridge, Suite 1000
McLean, VA 22102
Tel: 703-821-0770
Web: http://www.affi.com/

For information on careers, education, scholarships, and student memberships, contact:

Institute of Food Technologists
221 North LaSalle Street, Suite 300
Chicago, IL 60601-1291
Tel: 312-782-8424
Web: http://www.ift.org

For information on the industry and safety issues, contact:

National Food Processors Association
1350 I Street, NW, Suite 300
Washington, DC 20005
Tel: 202-639-5900
Web: http://www.nfpa-food.org

Commodities Brokers

School Subjects
Business
Mathematics

Personal Skills
Communication/ideas
Leadership/management

Work Environment
Primarily indoors
Primarily one location

Minimum Education Level
High school diploma

Salary Range
$22,660 to $48,090
to $1,000,000+

Certification or Licensing
Required by all states

Outlook
Much faster than the average

Overview

Commodities brokers, also known as *futures commission merchants*, act as agents in carrying out purchases and sales of commodities for customers or traders. Commodities are primary goods that are either raw or partially refined. Such goods are produced by farmers, such as corn, wheat, or cattle, or mined from the earth, such as gold, copper, or silver. Brokers, who may work at a brokerage house, on the floor of a commodities exchange, or independently, are paid a fee or commission for acting as the middleman to conduct and complete the trade.

History

In medieval Europe, business was transacted at local market fairs, and commodities, primarily agricultural, were traded at scheduled times and places. As market fairs grew, "fair letters" were set up as a currency representing a future cash settlement for a transaction. With these letters, merchants could travel from one fair to another. This was the precursor to the Japanese system in which landowners used "certificates of receipt" for their rice crops. As the certificates made their way into the economy, the Dojima Rice Market was established and became the first place where traders bought and sold contracts for the future delivery of rice. "Forward contracts" entered the U.S. marketplace in the early 19th century. Farmers, swept up in the boom of industrial growth, transportation, and commerce, began to arrange for the future sale of their crops. Traders entered the market along with the development of these contracts. However, there were no regulations to oversee that the commodity was actually delivered or that it was of an acceptable quality. Furthermore, each transaction was an individual business deal because the terms of each contract were variable. To address these issues, The Chicago Board of Trade was formed in 1848, and by 1865 had set up standards and rules for trading "to arrive" contracts, now known as commodity futures contracts.

The Job

A futures contract is an agreement to deliver a particular commodity, such as wheat, pork bellies, or coffee, at a specific date, time, and place. For example, farmers might sell their oats before they are sowed (known as "hedging") because the future selling price for their crops is unpredictable.If weather is favorable and crops are good, farmers face more competition, which will drive prices down. If there is a flood or drought, oats will be scarce, driving the selling price up. Farmers want to ensure a fair price for their products to protect business and limit risk.

On the other side of the equation is the user of the oats, perhaps a cereal manufacturer, who purchases these contracts for a delivery of oats at some future date. The third party is the *speculator*, or *trader*, who is neither a producer or consumer. Traders enter the market to make a profit by anticipating the direction of the commodity's price. Producers and consumers do not correspond to a one-to-one ratio, and it is the trader who acts as the middleman in the buying and selling of contracts.

Brokers place the trades of speculators who cannot place their own if they are not a member of an exchange. Brokers are paid a fee or commission for acting as the agent in making the sale. There are two broad categories of brokers, though they are becoming less distinct. *Full service brokers* provide considerable research to clients, offer price quotes, give trading advice, and assist the customer in making trading decisions. *Discount brokers* simply fill the orders as directed by clients. Some brokers offer intermediate levels of optional services on a sliding scale of commission, such as market research and strategic advice.

In general, brokers are responsible for taking and carrying out all commodity orders and being available on call to do so; reporting back to the client upon fulfilling the order request; keeping the client abreast of breaking news; maintaining account balances and other financial data; and obtaining market information when needed and informing the client about important changes in the marketplace.

Brokers can work on the floor of a commodity futures exchange—the marketplace where contracts are bought and sold—for a brokerage house, or independently. The exchange houses the trading floor where brokers transact their business in the trading pit. There are 11 domestic exchanges, with the main ones in Chicago, Kansas City, New York, and Minneapolis. A broker or trader must be a member of an exchange, which is a private membership organization. Membership is limited to a specific and small number of individuals who must purchase or rent a seat on the floor, which is quite expensive. Purchasing a seat on the Chicago Exchange, for example, costs $760,000 and also entails a thorough investigation of the applicant's credit standing, financial background, and character. Most brokers, therefore, work for a brokerage house dealing in futures. These may be companies like Merrill Lynch or Dean Witter, which deal in stocks, bonds, commodities, and other investments, or smaller houses such as R.J. O'Brien, which handle only commodities.

Companies can also have a seat on the exchange, and they have their own floor brokers in the pit to carry out trades for the brokerage house. Brokers in the company take orders from the public for buying or selling a contract and promptly pass it on to the *floor broker* in the pit of the exchange. Brokers also have the choice of running their own business. Known as *introducing brokers*, they handle their own clients and trades and use brokerage houses to place their orders. Introducing brokers earn a fee by soliciting business trades, but they don't directly handle the customer's funds.

Requirements

High School

Although there are no formal educational requirments for becoming a broker, a high school and a college degree are strongly recommended. Commodities brokers need to have a wide range of knowledge, covering such areas as economics, world politics, and sometimes even the weather. To begin to develop this broad base of knowledge, start in high school by taking history, math, science, and business classes. Since commodities brokers are constantly working with people to make a sale, take English classes to enhance your communication skills. In addition to this course work, you might also consider getting a part-time job working in a sales position. Such a job will also give you the chance to hone your communication and sales skills.

Postsecondary Training

The vast majority of brokers have a college degree. While there is no major specifically designed for commodities brokers, you can improve your chances of obtaining a job in this field by studying economics, finance, or business administration while in college. Keep in mind that you should continue to develop your understanding of politics and technologies, so government and computer classes will also be useful.

Brokerage firms look for employees who have sales ability, strong communication skills, and self-confidence. Commodities is often a second career for many people who have demonstrated these qualities in other positions.

Certification or Licensing

To become a commodities broker, it is necessary to pass the National Commodities Futures Examination (the Series 3 exam) to become eligible to satisfy the registration requirements of federal, state, and industry regulatory agencies. The test covers market and trading knowledge, as well as rules and regulations. The test costs $75 and is available through the National Futures Association. The Commodity Education Institute offers week-long courses to prepare for the exam. Brokers must also register with the National Futures Association. Floor brokers, however, are not required to take the exam and are instead put through a rigorous training program at the exchange.

Other Requirements

Brokers must possess a combination of research and money management skills. They need to be attentive to detail and have a knack for analyzing data. Strong communications and sales skills are important as well, as brokers make money by convincing people to let them place their trades. An interest in and awareness of the world around them is also a contributing factor to a broker's success, as commodities are influenced by everything from political decisions and international news to social and fashion trends.

Brokers must also be emotionally stable to work in such a volatile environment. They need to be persistent, aggressive, and comfortable taking risks and dealing with failure. Strong, consistent, and independent judgment is also key. Brokers must be disciplined hard workers, able to comb through reams of market reports and charts to gain a thorough understanding of their particular commodity and the mechanics of the marketplace. They also need to be outspoken and assertive, able to yell out prices loudly and energetically on the trading floor and command attention.

Exploring

Students interested in commodities trading should visit one of the futures exchanges. All of them offer public tours, and you'll get to see up close just how the markets work and the roles of the players involved. All the exchanges offer educational programs and publications, and most have a page on the World Wide Web (See *For More Information*). The Chicago Mercantile Exchange publishes *The Merc at Work*, the full text of which is also available on the Internet, as well as many other educational handbooks and pamphlets. There are hundreds of industry newsletters and magazines available (such as *Futures Magazine*), and many offer free samples of publications or products. Read what trading advisors have to say and how they say it. Learn their lingo and gain an understanding of the marketplace. If you have any contacts in the industry, arrange to spend a day with a broker. Watch him or her work, and you'll learn how orders are entered, processed, and reported.

Do your own research. Adopt a commodity, chart its prices, test some of your own ideas, and analyze the marketplace. There are also a variety of inexpensive software programs, as well as sites on the Web, that simulate trading.

Finally, consider a job as a runner during the summer before your freshman year in college. *Runners* transport the order, or "paper" from the phone clerk to the broker in the pit and relay information to and from members on the floor. This is the single best way to get hands-on experience in the industry.

Employers

Commodities brokers work on the floor of a commodity futures exchange, for brokerage houses, or independently.

Starting Out

College graduates can start working with a brokerage house as an associate and begin handling stocks. After several years they can take the certification exam and move into futures. Another option is to start as support staff, either at the exchange or the brokerage house. Sales personnel try to get customers to open accounts, and account executives develop and service customers for the brokerage firm. At the exchange, phone clerks receive incoming orders and communicate the information to the runners. Working in the back as an accountant, money manager, or member of the research staff is also another route. School placement offices may be able to assist graduates in finding jobs with brokerage houses. Applications may also be made directly to brokerage houses themselves.

Many successful brokers and traders began their careers as a runner, and each exchange has its own training program. Though the pay is low, runners learn the business very quickly with a hands-on experience not available in an academic classroom. Contact one of the commodities exchanges for information on becoming a runner.

Advancement

A broker who simply executes trades can advance to become a full-service broker. Through research and analysis and the accumulation of experience and knowledge about the industry, a broker can advance from an *order filler* and become a *commodity trading advisor*. A broker can also become a *money manager* and make all trading decisions for clients.

Within the exchange, a broker can become a *floor manager*, overseeing the processes of order-taking and information exchange. To make more money, a broker can also begin to place his or her own trades for his or her own private account, though the broker's first responsibility is to the customers.

Earnings

This is an entrepreneurial business. A broker's commission is based on the number of clients he or she recruits, the more they invest, and the amount of money they make. The sky's the limit. In recent years the most successful broker made $25 million. A typical salary for a newly hired employee in a brokerage might average $1,500 per month plus a 30 percent commission on sales. Smaller firms are likely to pay a smaller commission. The U.S. Department of Labor reports that the median annual earnings for securities, commodities, and financial services sales representatives were $48,090 in 1998. The lowest 10 percent earned less than $22,600; the highest 10 percent earned more than $124,800 annually.

Working with the Chicago Board of Trade, the world's leading futures exchange, offers numerous benefits. Employees are eligible for vacation six months after employment and receive three weeks after three years. Employees are also paid for sick days, personal days, and eight holidays. During the summer months various departments offer flex time, allowing employees to take Fridays off by working longer hours during the week. Employees also receive numerous forms of insurance, including medical, life, and disability. Full tuition reimbursement is available as is a company-matched savings plan, a tax-deferred savings plan, and a pension program. Other large exchanges and brokerage houses offer similar combinations of benefits.

Work Environment

The trading floor is noisy and chaotic, as trading is done using an "open outcry" system. Every broker must be an auctioneer, yelling out his own price bids for purchases and sales. The highest bid wins and silences all the others. When a broker's primal scream is not heard, bids and offers can also be communicated with hand signals.

Brokers stand for most of the day, often in the same place, so that traders interested in their commodity can locate them easily. Each broker wears a distinctly colored jacket with a prominent identification badge. The letter on the badge identifies the broker and appears on the paperwork relating to the trade. Members of the exchange and employees of member firms wear red jackets. Some brokers and traders also have uniquely patterned jackets to further increase their visibility in the pit.

Brokers and traders do not have a nine-to-five job. While commodities trading on the exchange generally takes place from 9 AM to 1 PM, international trading runs from 2:45 PM to 6:50 AM.

In the rough and tumble world of the futures exchange, emotions run high as people often win or lose six-figure amounts within hours. Tension is fierce, the pace is frantic, and angry, verbal, and sometimes physical exchanges are not uncommon.

Outlook

The U.S. Bureau of Labor Statistics predicts much faster than the average growth—about 41 percent—for securities and financial sales representatives through 2008. Two major trends are affecting the future of the commodities industry: international growth and new technology. Though the industry on the whole is small (50,000 firms as compared to the 400,000 firms in securities) and firms are sizing down, the number of exchanges has doubled in the last 10 years, and in 1998 there were 68 exchanges in 28 countries. The United States used to control 90 percent of the world's business, and now accounts for just 45 percent. Opportunities to manage commodities are no longer limited to the United States.

New commodities are also bursting onto the scene. During the 1980s, 186 new futures contracts were introduced. And nearly half of the total volume of trades were a product of these new contracts. Look for new types of commodities to continue to grow along with the move toward globalization, and for brokers to become highly specialized.

New computer and information technology is rapidly influencing and advancing the industry. A growing number of exchanges now use electronic systems to automate trades, and many use them exclusively. Many systems have unique features designed specifically to meet customers' needs. New technology, such as electronic order entry, hookups to overseas exchanges, and night trading, is rapidly evolving, offering brokers new ways to manage risk and provide price information.

For More Information

This center provides information on workshops, home study courses, educational materials, and publications for futures and securities professionals.

Center for Futures Education
410 Erie Street
PO Box 309
Grove City, PA 16127
Tel: 724-458-5860
Email: info@thectr.com
Web: http://www.thectr.com/

For a history of CBOT, and information on tours and educational programs, contact:

Chicago Board of Trade (CBOT)
141 West Jackson Boulevard
Chicago, IL 60604-2994
Tel: 312-435-3500
Web: http://www.cbot.com

For an overview of options, visit the Education section of the CBOE Web site.

Chicago Board Options Exchange (CBOE)
400 South LaSalle Street
Chicago, IL 60605
Email: help@cboe.com
Web: http://www.cboe.com

The Chicago Mercantile Exchange offers a wide variety of educational programs and materials, and general information on commodities careers through the Educational Resources section of its Web site.

Chicago Mercantile Exchange
30 South Wacker Drive
Chicago, IL 60606
Tel: 312-930-1000
Email: edu@cme.com
Web: http://www.cme.com

For information on the NASD Institute for Professional Development, contact:

National Association of Securities Dealers (NASD)
33 Whitehall Street, 8th Floor
New York, NY 10004
Tel: 212-858-4000
Web: http://www.nasd.com/

For information on registration and the National Commodities Futures Examination, contact:

National Futures Association
200 West Madison Street, Suite 1600
Chicago, IL 60606
Tel: 800-621-3570
Email: public_affairs@nfa.futures.org
Web: http://www.nfa.futures.org/

The Educational section of the Philadelphia Board of Trade's Web site provides a glossary of terms, suggested reading, and an overview of the financial industry.

Philadelphia Board of Trade
1900 Market Street
Philadelphia, PA 19103-3584
Tel: 800-THE-PHLX
Email: info@phlx.com
Web: http://www.phlx.com

Visit the Web sites or contact the following exchanges for general background information about the field.

Coffee, Sugar & Cocoa Exchange, Inc.
4 World Trade Center
New York, NY 10048
Tel: 212-742-6000
Web: http://www.csce.com

MidAmerica Commodity Exchange
141 West Jackson Boulevard
Chicago, IL 60604
Tel: 312-341-3000
Web: http://www.midam.com

Minneapolis Grain Exchange
400 South 4th Street
Minneapolis, MN 55415
Tel: 800-827-4746
Email: info@mgex.com
Web: http://www.mgex.com

New York Futures Exchange
4 World Trade Center
New York, NY 10048
Tel: 212-938-2626
Web: http://www.nybot.com

New York Mercantile Exchange
NYMEX/COMEX
One North End Avenue
World Financial Center
New York, NY 10282-1101
Tel: 212-299-2000
Email: exchangeinfo@nymex.com
Web: http://www.nymex.com

Dairy Products Manufacturing Workers

School Subjects
Agriculture
Chemistry

Personal Skills
Following instructions
Technical/scientific

Work Environment
Primarily indoors
Primarily one location

Minimum Education Level
High school diploma

Salary Range
$15,000 to $27,500 to $40,000+

Certification or Licensing
Required by all states

Outlook
Decline

Overview

Dairy products manufacturing workers set up, operate, and tend continuous-flow or vat-type equipment to process milk, cream, butter, cheese, ice cream, and other dairy products following specified methods and formulas.

History

Since herd animals were first domesticated, humankind has kept cattle for meat and milk. From its ancient beginnings in Asia, the practice of keeping cattle spread across much of the world. Often farmers kept a few cows to supply their family's dairy needs. Because fresh milk spoils easily, milk that was not consumed as a beverage had to be made into a product like cheese. Before the invention of refrigeration, cheese was the only dairy product that could be easily transported across long distances. Over the centuries, many distinctive types of hard cheeses have become associated with various regions of the world, such as Cheddar from England, Edam and Gouda from Holland, Gruyere from Switzerland, and Parmesan and Provolone from Italy.

A real dairy products industry has developed only in the last century or so, with the development of refrigeration and various kinds of specialized processing machinery, the scientific study of cattle breeding, and improved road and rail transportation systems for distributing manufactured products. The rise in urban populations also gave an extra impetus to the growth of the industry, as more and more people moved away from farm sources of dairy products and into cities.

Another important development was the introduction of pasteurization, named for the noted French chemist Louis Pasteur (1822-95). Many harmful bacteria can live in fresh milk. In the 1860s, Pasteur developed the process of pasteurization, which involves heating a foodstuff to a certain temperature for a specified period of time to kill the bacteria, then cooling the food again.

The Job

Dairy products manufacturing workers handle a wide variety of machines that process milk, manufacture dairy products, and prepare the products for shipping. Workers are usually classified by the type of machine they operate. Workers at some plants handle more than one type of machine.

Whole milk is delivered to a dairy processing plant from farms in large containers or in special tank trucks. The milk is stored in large vats until *dairy processing equipment operators* are ready to use it. First, the operator connects the vats to processing equipment with pipes, assembling whatever valves, bowls, plates, disks, impeller shafts, and other parts are needed to prepare the equipment for operation. Then the operator turns valves to pump a sterilizing solution and rinse water throughout the pipes and equipment. While keeping an eye on temperature and pressure gauges, the operator opens other valves to pump the whole milk into a centrifuge where it is spun at high speed to separate the cream from the skim milk. The milk is also pumped through a homogenizer to produce a specified emulsion (consistency that results from the distribution of fat through the milk) and, last, through a filter to remove any sediment. All this is done through continuous-flow machines.

The next step for the equipment operator is pasteurization, or the killing of bacteria that exist in the milk. The milk is heated by pumping steam or hot water through pipes in the pasteurization equipment. When it has been at the specified temperature for the correct length of time, a refrigerant is pumped through refrigerator coils in the equipment, which quickly brings the milk temperature down. Once the milk has been pasteurized, it is either bottled in glass, paper, or plastic containers, or it is pumped to other storage tanks for further processing. The dairy processing equipment operator may also add to the milk specified amounts of liquid or powdered ingredients, such as vitamins, lactic culture, stabilizer, or neutralizer, to make products such as buttermilk, yogurt, chocolate milk, or ice cream. The batch of milk is tested for acidity at various stages of this process, and each time the operator records the time, temperature, pressure, and volume readings for the milk. The operator may clean the equipment before processing the next batch of whole milk.

Processed milk includes a lot of nonfat dry milk, which is far easier to ship and store than fresh milk. Dry milk is produced in a gas-fired drier tended by a *drier operator*. The drier operator first turns on the equipment's drier mechanism, vacuum pump, and circulating fan and adjusts the flow controls. Once the proper drier temperature is reached, a pump sprays liquid milk into the heated vacuum chamber where milk droplets dry to powder and fall to the bottom of the chamber. The drier operator tests the dried powder for the proper moisture content and the chamber walls for burnt scale, which indicates excessive temperatures and appears as undesirable sediment when the milk is reconstituted. *Milk-powder grinders* operate equipment that mills and sifts the milk powder, ensuring a uniform texture.

For centuries, butter was made by hand in butter churns in which cream was agitated with a plunger until pieces of butter congealed and separated from the milk. Modern butter-making machines perform the same basic operation on a much larger scale. After sterilizing the machine, the *butter maker* starts a pump that admits a measured amount of pasteurized cream into the churn. The butter maker activates the churn and, as the cream is agitated by paddles, monitors the gradual separation of the butter from the milk. Once the process is complete, the milk is pumped out and stored, and the butter is sprayed with chlorinated water to remove excess remaining milk. With testing apparatus, the butter maker determines the butter's moisture and salt content and adjusts the consistency by adding or removing water. Finally, the butter maker examines the color and smells and tastes the butter to grade it according to predetermined standards.

In addition to the churn method, butter can also be produced by a chilling method. In this process, the butter maker pasteurizes and separates cream to obtain butter oil. The butter oil is tested in a standardizing vat for its levels of butter fat, moisture, salt content, and acidity. The butter maker adds appropriate amounts of water, alkali, and coloring to the butter oil and starts an agitator to mix the ingredients. The resulting mix is chilled in a vat at a specified temperature until it congeals into butter.

Cheesemakers cook milk and other ingredients according to formulas to make cheese. The cheesemaker first fills a cooking vat with milk of a prescribed butterfat content, heats the milk to a specified temperature, and dumps in measured amounts of dye and starter culture. The mixture is agitated and tested for acidity, which affects the rate at which enzymes coagulate milk proteins and produce cheese. When a certain level of acidity has been reached, the cheesemaker adds a measured amount of rennet, a substance containing milk-curdling enzymes. The milk is left alone to coagulate into curd, the thick, protein-rich part of milk used to make cheese. The cheesemaker later releases the whey, the watery portion of the milk, by pulling curd knives through the curd or using a hand scoop. Then the curd is agitated in the vat and cooked for a period of time, with the cheesemaker squeezing and stretching samples of curd by hand and adjusting the cooking time to achieve the desired firmness or texture. Once this is done, the cheesemaker drains the whey from the curd, adds ingredients such as seasonings, and then molds, packs, cuts, piles, mills, and presses the curd into specified shapes. To make certain types of cheese, the curd may be immersed in brine, rolled in dry salt, pierced or smeared with a culture solution to develop mold growth, or placed on shelves to be cured. Later, the cheesemaker samples the cheese for its taste, smell, look, and feel. Sampling and grading is also done by *cheese graders*, experts in cheeses who are required to have a state or federal license.

The distinctive qualities of various kinds of cheeses depend on a number of factors, including the kind and condition of the milk, the cheesemaking process, and the method and duration of curing. For example, cottage cheese is made by the method described above. However, the *cottage cheese maker* starts the temperature low and slowly increases it. When the curd reaches the proper consistency, the cottage cheese maker stops the cooking process and drains off the whey. This method accounts for cottage cheese's loose consistency. Cottage cheese and other soft cheeses are not cured like hard cheeses and are meant for immediate consumption.

Process cheese products are made by blending and cooking different cheeses, cheese curd, or other ingredients such as cream, vegetable shortening, sodium citrate, and disodium phosphate. The *process cheese cooker* dumps the various ingredients into a vat and cooks them at a prescribed temperature. When the mixture reaches a certain consistency, the cooker pulls a lever to drain the cheese into a hopper or bucket. The process cheese may be pumped through a machine that makes its texture finer. Unheated cheese or curd may be mixed with other ingredients to make cold pack cheese or cream cheese. Other cheese workers include *casting-machine operators*, who tend the machines that form, cool, and cut the process cheese into slices of a specified size and weight, and *grated-cheese makers,* who handle the grinding, drying, and cooling equipment that makes grated cheese.

Ice cream is usually made from milk fat, nonfat milk solids, sweeteners, stabilizer (usually gelatin), and flavorings such as syrup, nuts, and fruit. Ice cream can be made in individual batches by *batch freezers* or in continuous-mix equipment by *freezer operators*. In the second method, the freezer operator measures the dry and liquid ingredients, such as the milk, coloring, flavoring, or fruit puree, and dumps them into the flavor vat. The mix is blended, pumped into freezer barrels, and injected with air. In the freezer barrel, the mix is agitated and scraped from the freezer walls while it slowly hardens. The operator then releases the ice cream through a valve outlet that may inject flavored syrup for rippled ice cream. The ice cream is transferred to a filling machine that pumps it into cartons, cones, cups, or molds for pies, rolls, and tarts. Other workers may process the ice cream into its various types, such as cones, varicolored packs, and special shapes. These workers include decorators, novelty makers, flavor room workers, and sandwich-machine operators.

Newly hired inexperienced workers in a dairy processing plant may start out as dairy helpers, cheesemaker helpers, or cheese making laborers. Beginning workers may do any of a wide variety of support tasks, such as scrubbing and sterilizing bottles and equipment, attaching pipes and fittings to machines, packing cartons, weighing containers, and moving stock. If they prove to be reliable, workers may be given more responsibility and assigned tasks such as filling tanks with milk or ingredients, examining canned milk for dirt or odor, monitoring machinery, cutting and wrapping butter and cheese, or filling cartons or bags with powdered milk. In time, workers may be trained to operate and repair any of the specialized processing machines found in the factory.

The raw milk at a dairy processing plant is supplied by *dairy farmers*, who raise and tend milk-producing livestock, usually cows. Dairy farmers often own their own farms, breed their own cows, and use special equipment to milk the cows, often twice a day. Many also perform other farm-related tasks, including growing crops. Assisting the dairy farmer is often the *dairy herd supervisor*, who takes milk samples from cows and tests the milk samples for information such as the amount of fat, protein, and other solids present in the milk. The dairy herd supervisor helps the farmer make certain that each cow in the herd is healthy and that the milk they produce will be fit for human consumption. Dairy herd supervisors do not generally work for one dairy farmer, but rather may oversee the milk production at a number of farms.

Requirements

High School

Most dairy products manufacturing workers learn their skills from company training sessions and on-the-job experience. Employers prefer to hire workers with at least a high school education. Courses that can provide helpful background for work in this field include mathematics, biology, and chemistry. Machine shop classes also can be useful for the experience gained in handling and repairing heavy machinery.

Postsecondary Training

Students interested in becoming cheesemakers may find it necessary to obtain a college degree in a food technology or food science program. Dairy herd supervisors, in addition to a two-year or four-year food technology or food science degree, should try to gain experience working on a dairy farm. Those who seek management positions may need a bachelor's degree in food manufacturing with an emphasis on accounting, management, and other business courses.

Certification or Licensing

To ensure that consumers are receiving safe, healthful dairy foods, many dairy products manufacturing workers must be licensed by a state board of health or other local government unit. Licensing is intended to guarantee workers' knowledge of health laws, their skills in handling equipment, and their ability to grade the quality of various goods according to established standards. Some workers, such as cheese graders, may need to be licensed by the federal government as well.

Other Requirements

Many dairy manufacturing workers must pass physical examinations and receive certificates stating they are free from contagious diseases. An interest in food products and manual dexterity in operating equipment are important characteristics for this work.

Exploring

People who think they may be interested in working in the dairy products manufacturing industry may be able to find summer jobs as helpers in dairy processing plants. Assisting or at least observing equipment operators, cheesemakers, butter makers, and others as they work is a good way to learn about this field. High school students may also find part-time or summer employment at dairy farms.

Starting Out

A good place to find information about job openings is at the personnel offices of local dairy processing plants. Other sources of information include newspaper classified ads and the offices of the state employment service. Those with associate's or bachelor's degrees in food technology, food science, or a related program can apply directly to dairy processing plants; many schools offering such programs provide job placement assistance. Dairy farmers often begin their careers by working on their own family farms.

Advancement

After gaining some experience, dairy products manufacturing workers may advance to become shift supervisors or production supervisors. Advancement is usually limited to those with at least an associate's or bachelor's degree in a food technology, food science, or related course of study. Formal training in related fields is necessary in order to move up to such positions as laboratory technician, plant engineer, or plant manager.

Workers who wish to change industries may find that many of their skills can be transferred to other types of food processing. With further training and education, they may eventually become dairy plant inspectors or technicians employed by local or state health departments.

Earnings

Earnings of dairy products manufacturing workers vary widely according to the responsibilities of the worker, geographical location, and other factors. Entry-level and unskilled workers can expect to begin at salaries around $15,000 per year. Dairy production workers with experience averaged approximately $27,500 per year in 1995. The overall average earnings for dairy production workers also varies according to the type of product produced by the plant. Workers processing fluid milk earned an average of $28,700 per year, while those at cheese processing plants averaged about $24,400 per year. Cheesemakers and others with food technology degrees may earn as much as $40,000 per year or more. Production supervisors, plant engineers, and plant managers can earn $30,000 per year or more. Annual income for dairy farmers can vary widely, from as low as $10,000 per year to $90,000 per year and more; most dairy farmers own their own businesses and are responsible for its upkeep, as well as paying employees' salaries.

Dairy herd supervisors are paid based on the number of herd they test. Starting supervisors earn between $18,700 and $25,000, while experienced supervisors may earn $30,000 per year. The most experienced and highly trained supervisors can earn as much as $35,000 per year. Most dairy products workers are eligible for overtime pay for hours worked over 40 hours in a week. Benefits vary according to the company and its location, but sometimes include health insurance and vacation and sick pay.

Work Environment

Because of the strict health codes and sanitary standards to which they must adhere, dairy plants are generally clean, well-ventilated workplaces, equipped with modern, well-maintained machines. When workplace safety rules are followed, dairy processing plants are not hazardous places to work.

Workers in this industry generally report for work as early as 6 AM, with shifts ending around three in the afternoon. Dairy farmers and others may start work as early as four or five in the morning. People involved in the agriculture industry often work very long hours, often more than 12 hours per day. Many dairy products manufacturing workers stand during most of their workday. In some positions the work is very repetitive. Although the milk itself is generally transported from tank to tank via pipelines, some workers have to lift and carry other heavy items, such as cartons of flavoring, emulsifier, chemical additives, and finished products like cheese. To clean vats and other equipment, some workers have to get inside storage tanks and spray the walls with hot water, chemicals, or live steam.

Outlook

In 1998, there were 15,000 workers employed in this industry. The demand for American dairy products will probably remain high in the foreseeable future. Among the products that have grown in popularity in recent years are cheeses, ice cream, and lowfat milk. Despite this demand, employment in the dairy products manufacturing industry is expected to decline between 1998 and 2008, according to the *Occupational Outlook Handbook*. Improvements in technology and increased automation are two important factors contributing to this trend. However, because the milk industry is rarely affected by recessions or other economic difficulties and trends facing other industries, employment remains relatively stable and this industry suffers fewer layoffs than others. Because of continuing advances in the technology of dairy manufacturing and food science, the demand for laboratory technicians, plant engineers, and other technical staff is expected to remain strong.

For More Information

For information about the dairy industry, contact:

American Dairy Association
2015 Rice Street
Saint Paul, MN 55113
Tel: 651-488-0261
Email: info@midwestdairy.com
Web: http://www.dairycenter.com/

The following organization has a journal, a student affiliate, and information about the dairy industry.

American Dairy Science Association
1111 North Dunlap Avenue
Savoy, IL 61874
Tel: 217-356-3182
Email: adsa@assochq.org
Web: http://www.adsa.uiuc.edu

The following is a federation of the Milk Industry Foundation, National Cheese Institute, and the International Ice Cream Association.

International Dairy Foods Association
1250 H Street, NW, Suite 900
Washington, DC 20005
Tel: 202-737-4332
Web: http://www.idfa.org

The following organization is concerned with milk quality and standards, animal health and food safety issues, dairy product labeling and standards, and legislation affecting the dairy industry.

National Milk Producers Federation
2101 Wilson Boulevard, Suite 400
Arlington, VA 22201
Tel: 703-243-6111
Email: nmpf@aol.com
Web: http://www.nmpf.org

Farm Crop Production Technicians

School Subjects

Business
Earth science

Personal Skills

Leadership/management
Technical/scientific

Work Environment

Indoors and outdoors
Primarily multiple locations

Minimum Education Level

Some postsecondary training

Salary Range

$14,140 to $23,467 to $34,370

Certification or Licensing

Required for certain positions

Outlook

Decline

Overview

Farm crop production technicians are involved with farmers and agricultural businesses in all aspects of planting, growing, and marketing crops. With backgrounds in agriculture and scientific research, they advise farmers on how best to produce crops. They may also work for companies that produce agricultural products such as fertilizer and equipment to make sure they are meeting the needs of farmers.

History

Until the early 20th century, crops were planted, maintained, and harvested by individual farmers. During harvest, farmers may have called upon the assistance of neighboring farmers or local work crews, but most aspects of crop production were handled by family members. The typical family farm measured about 160 acres. Horses were used to power simple machinery that was repaired, and oftentimes built, by the farmers themselves. Although the family farm once stood as a symbol of independent living, the demands of production throughout the 20th century called upon the skills, talents, and labors of others.

Advances in equipment technology, methods of conservation, and pesticides and fertilizers led to more farm output, but also fewer family farms. By 1950, the average farm had grown greatly in size and needed to be highly efficient in order to turn a profit. Farm owners began to rely on outside assistance in crop production, and those with farm experience, but without their own farms, found new career opportunities in crop production assistance. Agribusiness developed in the 1960s to help farmers with the complicated process of managing a farm crop, from the selecting of seed to the marketing of the final product. Today, technicians, engineers, scientists, conservationists, and government agencies work together to help farms stay profitable and produce crops for a global market.

The Job

Corn, soybeans, wheat, cotton, fruit—these are some of the top crops in the agricultural industry. The farms and orchards that produce these crops have very specific needs, differing from the needs of livestock and dairy farms. Those with an understanding of how to best prepare soil, treat plants, and harvest, work as farm crop production technicians. These technicians may have different employers, from scientists to government agencies to the farmers themselves, but they share intentions—to use their knowledge of crops and production to help farmers increase yields and market their products. And the work can be varied, involving grading and handling, pest and disease control, finding new uses for crops, and similar tasks.

Nearly everything used on a farm is now purchased from outside suppliers: seed, fertilizer, pesticides, machinery, fuels, and general supplies. Companies selling these products need farm-trained and farm-oriented technicians who can understand buyers' farming problems and needs. Farm supply companies also need technicians to assist in research and development. These technicians work under the supervision of feed or chemical company scientists, carrying out the details of the testing program.

In the production phase of crop technology, some technicians make soil or tissue tests to determine the efficiency of fertilizer programs. Others are responsible for the maintenance of farm machinery. More experienced farm crop production technicians may oversee the complete management of a farm, including personnel, machinery, and finances.

Practically all agricultural products need some processing before they reach the consumer. Processing involves testing, grading, packaging, and transporting. Some of the technicians in this area work closely with farmers and need to know a great deal about crop production. For example, *field-contact technicians* employed by food-processing companies monitor crop production on the farms from which they buy products. In some processing companies, technicians supervise the entire crop operation. In others, they act as buyers or determine when crops will be harvested for processing and shipping.

Some technicians may work for the government or businesses performing quality-control work or nutrition research; others work as inspectors. This work is usually done in a laboratory.

In addition to the positions mentioned above, farm crop production technicians may take on the following titles and responsibilities.

Processing and distributing technicians may find jobs with canneries, freezing and packing plants, cooperatives, or distributors to make sure the work is up to government standards and to advise on matters of efficiency and profitability. They may work either in the laboratory or in the field with the grower. The laboratory technician works with a scientist to maintain quality control, test, grade, measure, and keep records. The field technician supervises seed selection and planting, weed and pest control, irrigation, harvesting, and on-the-spot testing to make sure crops are harvested at precisely the right state of maturity.

Seed production field supervisors help coordinate the activities of farmers who produce seed for commercial seed companies. They inspect and analyze soil and water supplies for farms and study other growing conditions in order to plan production of planted crops. They distribute seed stock to farmers, specify areas and numbers of acres to be planted, and give instructions to workers engaged in cultivation procedures, such as fertilization, tilling, and detasseling. They may also determine dates and methods for harvesting, storing, and shipping seed crops.

Agricultural inspectors work for state, county, and federal departments of agriculture. In order to inspect grain, vegetables, or seed, they must know grades and standards and be able to recognize common pests and disease damage. They may work in the field, at a packing shed or shipping station, or at a terminal market.

Biological aides assist research workers in biology, bacteriology, plant pathology, mycology, and related agricultural sciences. They set up laboratory and field equipment, perform routine tests, and clean up and maintain field and laboratory equipment. They also keep records of plant growth, experimental plots, greenhouse activity, insecticide use, and other agricultural experimentation.

Disease and insect control field inspectors inspect fields to detect the presence of harmful insects and plant diseases. Inspectors count the numbers of insects on plants or of diseased plants within a sample area. They record the results of their counts on field work sheets. They also collect samples of unidentifiable insects or diseased plants for identification by a supervisor.

Spray equipment operators work for pest-control companies. They select and apply the proper herbicides or pesticides for particular jobs, formulate mixtures, and operate various types of spraying and dusting equipment. A specialized technician within this occupation is the aircraft crop duster or sprayer.

Requirements

High School

You should take courses in mathematics and science; depending on your area of work, you'll need an understanding of biology and chemistry. You should complete as much vocational agriculture work as possible, including agricultural mechanics. In addition, English is very important, because much of the work requires good communication skills.

Postsecondary Training

A career as a farm crop production technician requires training in a rigorous two-year technical or agricultural college program in order to learn the principles of crop production. In such a training program, you can expect to take a broad range of courses relating to agriculture in general and farm crop production in particular, as well as some general education courses. Typical first-year courses include the following: agricultural machinery, animal husbandry, soil science, entomology, English, physical education, science, and mathematics. Typical second-year courses include agricultural economics, soil fertility, plant pathology, forage and seed crops, and social science.

If you wish to specialize in vegetable or fruit production, you may be able to modify your program to concentrate in these areas. You may study topics such as vegetable and fruit production in the first year and vegetable and fruit marketing in the second.

Certification or Licensing

The majority of technicians in the field are not required to have a license or certification. However, technicians involved in grading or inspecting for local, state, or federal government units must pass examinations to be qualified. Some other government jobs, such as that of research assistant, may also require a competitive examination.

Other Requirements

You'll need manual skills and mechanical ability to operate various kinds of equipment and machinery. You must also be able to apply scientific principles to the processing procedures, materials, and measuring and control devices found at the modern laboratory or farm. You must be able to communicate what needs to be done and interpret the orders you're given.

Exploring

Students who grow up on farms have the best opportunity to explore this field, but living on a farm is not the only way to check out this work. You can also join the local branch of the National FFA Organization (formerly Future Farmers of America) or a local 4-H club. These groups will give you the opportunity to work on farm projects and meet professionals in the field. You may also be able to obtain work experience on farms during the summer when extra labor is always required for planting, detasseling, and harvesting. During postsecondary training, heavy emphasis is placed on supervised occupational experience for students to become familiar with job requirements.

Employers

With a background in crop production, the farm crop production technician is able to find work in a variety of settings. Although some may work directly for farmers, most of these technicians work in businesses that support agriculture. They can work for feed and supply companies, inspection departments and other government agencies, nurseries, grain elevators, and farm equipment sales and service companies. They work under the supervision of agricultural scientists, farm managers, and agribusiness professionals.

Starting Out

Once you are in a postsecondary training program, you will be encouraged to decide as early as possible which phase of crop technology you prefer to enter, because contacts made while in school can be helpful in obtaining a job after the program's completion. You will find that students are often hired by the same firm they worked for during a work-study program. If that firm does not have a position open, a recommendation from the employer will help with other firms.

Most faculty members in a technical program have contact with prospective employers and can help place qualified students. You can also take advantage of your school's placement service, which should arrange interviews between students and prospective employers.

Advancement

Technicians in the field of farm crop production have many opportunities for advancement. Early advancement will be easier for those who combine a formal technical education with work experience. Those who have had several jobs in the industry will probably advance to managerial levels more rapidly than those who have not. As more postsecondary schools are established in local communities, it becomes easier for employed persons to continue their education through evening classes while they work. Although a bachelor's degree in agriculture may be required to advance to some positions, technicians may be able to substitute a great deal of experience for the degree.

Some technicians are able to become managers, supervisors, sales representatives, and agribusiness or farm owners.

Earnings

Salaries of farm crop production technicians vary widely. Technicians employed in off-the-farm jobs often receive higher salaries than technicians working on farms. Technicians working on farms, however, often receive food and housing benefits that can be the equivalent of several thousand dollars a year. Salaries also vary according to the geographic area with jobs in the northeast region being at the lower end of the scale and jobs in California, Minnesota, and Iowa at the upper end of the scale.

According to a 1998 salary survey conducted by AGRICAREERS, Inc., crop assistants made an average of $23,467 a year. Those on the low end of the wage scale received $18,000 annually; those on the high end, $30,000. Some technicians may receive salaries that are significantly above or below this range. The 1998 edition of the *O*Net Dictionary of Occupational Titles,* for example, reported that disease and insect control inspectors earned approximately $14,140 annually. Agricultural inspectors, on the other hand, had yearly earnings of approximately $34,370. Salaries are influenced by such factors as the technician's educational background, the technician's agricultural experience, and the type of crop involved. Health coverage and other benefits also depend on the position and employer.

Work Environment

Certain technicians in this field work primarily outdoors and must be able to adapt to extreme weather conditions. There may be certain seasons of the year when they are required to work long hours under considerable pressure to get a crop harvested or processed at just the right time.

The work of laboratory technicians in this field involves exacting, systematic procedures in facilities that are generally clean and comfortable. Inspection technicians may work long hours during harvest season. Work in the processing phase is usually indoors, except for the field-service or field-contact personnel, who spend much of their time outdoors.

Planting a new field, orchard, or vineyard, and watching it grow and develop, can be extremely rewarding. However, a stable temperament is essential when facing the continual uncertainties of weather conditions such as possible blight and premature frost and the possible loss of one's investment.

For technicians who feel they may lack some of these characteristics, employment in sales and services is advised. Here, too, on-the-job satisfaction can be found playing a vital role in producing humanity's most basic need.

Outlook

While farm products have not decreased in importance, the employment of farmers and farm managers today is on the decline as farms consolidate and become more mechanized. The U.S. Department of Labor predicts that employment for farm workers involved in food and fiber crop production will also decline through 2008. However, workers will be needed to replace those who leave the field, and organizations, such as the Peace Corps, can provide opportunities for agricultural technicians in the underdeveloped nations of the world.

For technicians interested specifically in orchard and vineyard production, the outlook may be somewhat brighter. Those technicians hoping to own or operate their own orchards or vineyards should remember, of course, that not all crops are necessarily good investments at all times. Local conditions, business cycles, and supply and demand must be considered when making decisions on the planting of a certain kind of orchard, grove, or vineyard.

For More Information

For a career resources booklet, contact:

American Society of Agronomy
677 South Segoe Road
Madison, WI 53711
Tel: 608-273-8080
Web: http://www.agronomy.org

For more information on education and opportunities in the agricultural field, contact:

4-H
Stop 2225
1400 Independence Avenue, SW
Washington, DC 20250-2225
Tel: 202-720-2908
Web: http://www.4h-usa.org

National FFA Organization
6060 FFA Drive
PO Box 68960
Indianapolis, IN 46268
Tel: 317-802-6060
Web: http://www.ffa.org

To read about research projects concerning crop production, visit the USDA Web site, or contact:

U.S. Department of Agriculture (USDA)
14th Street and Independence, SW
Washington, DC 20250
Tel: 202-720-2791
Web: http://www.usda.gov

Farm Equipment Mechanics

School Subjects

Agriculture
Technical/shop

Personal Skills

Mechanical/manipulative
Technical/scientific

Work Environment

Indoors and outdoors
Primarily multiple locations

Minimum Education Level

Some postsecondary training

Salary Range

$14,470 to $22,755 to $33,300

Certification or Licensing

None available

Outlook

Decline

Overview

Farm equipment mechanics maintain, adjust, repair, and overhaul equipment and vehicles used in planting, cultivating, harvesting, moving, processing, and storing plant and animal farm products. Among the specialized machines with which they work are tractors, harvesters, combines, pumps, tilling equipment, silo fillers, hay balers, and sprinkler irrigation systems. They work for farm equipment repair shops, farm equipment dealerships, and on large farms that have their own shops. Approximately 49,000 farm equipment mechanics work in the United States.

History

The purpose of the mechanical devices used in farming has always been to increase production and decrease the need for human labor. In prehistoric times, people used simple wood and stone implements to help turn soil, plant seeds, and harvest crops more efficiently than they could with their bare hands. With the introduction of metal tools and the domestication of animals that could pull plows and vehicles, people were able to produce much more. Until the 19th century, farmers around the globe relied on human labor, animal power, and relatively simple equipment to accomplish all the tasks involved in agriculture.

Modern mechanized agriculture was developed in the 1800s. Initially, steam power was used for farm equipment. In the early part of the 20th century, gasoline-powered engines appeared. Shortly after, diesel engines were introduced to power various kinds of farm machinery. The use of motor-driven machines on farms had far-reaching effects. Machines improved agricultural productivity while lessening the need for human labor. As a result of increased use of farm machinery, the number of people working on farms has steadily decreased in many countries of the world.

In recent decades, farm machines have become large and complex, using electronic, computerized, and hydraulic systems. Agriculture is now a business operation that requires extremely expensive equipment capable of doing specialized tasks quickly and efficiently. Farmers cannot afford for their equipment to break down. They are now almost completely reliant on the dealers who sell them their equipment to be their source for the emergency repairs and routine maintenance services that keep the machines functioning well. Farm equipment mechanics are the skilled specialists who carry out these tasks, usually as employees of equipment dealers or of independent repair shops.

The Job

The success of today's large-scale farming operations depends on the reliability of many complex machines. It is the farm equipment mechanic's responsibility to keep the machines in good working order and repair or to overhaul them when they break down.

When farm equipment is not working properly, mechanics begin by diagnosing the problem. Using intricate testing devices, they are able to identify what is wrong. A compression tester, for example, can determine whether cylinder valves leak or piston rings are worn, and a dynamometer can measure engine performance. The mechanic will also examine the machine, observing and listening to it in operation and looking for clues such as leaks, loose parts, and irregular steering, braking, and gear shifting. It may be necessary to dismantle whole systems in the machine to diagnose and correct malfunctions.

When the problem is located, the broken, worn-out, or faulty components are repaired or replaced, depending on the extent of their defect. The machine or piece of equipment is reassembled, adjusted, lubricated, and tested to be sure it is again operating at its full capacity.

Farm equipment mechanics use many tools in their work. Besides hand tools such as wrenches, pliers, and screwdrivers and precision instruments such as micrometers and torque wrenches, they may use welding equipment, power grinders and saws, and other power tools. In addition, they do major repairs using machine tools such as drill presses, lathes, and milling and woodworking machines.

As farm equipment becomes more complex, mechanics are increasingly expected to have strong backgrounds in electronics. For instance, newer tractors have large, electronically controlled engines and air-conditioned cabs, as well as transmissions with many speeds.

Much of the time, farmers can bring their equipment into a shop, where mechanics have all the necessary tools available. But during planting or harvesting seasons, when timing may be critical for the farmers, mechanics are expected to travel to farms for emergency repairs in order to get the equipment up and running with little delay.

Farmers usually bring movable equipment into a repair shop on a regular basis for preventive maintenance services such as adjusting and cleaning parts and tuning engines. Routine servicing not only ensures less emergency repairs for the mechanics, but it also assures farmers that the equipment will be ready when it is needed. Shops in the rural outskirts of metropolitan areas often handle maintenance and repairs on a variety of lawn and garden equipment, especially lawn mowers.

If a mechanic works in a large shop, he or she may specialize in specific types of repairs. For example, a mechanic may overhaul gasoline or diesel engines, repair clutches and transmissions, or concentrate on the air-conditioning units in the cabs of combines and large tractors. Some mechanics, called *farm machinery set-up mechanics*, uncrate, assemble, adjust, and often deliver machinery to farm locations. Mechanics also do body work on tractors and other machines, repairing damaged sheet metal body parts.

Some mechanics may work exclusively on certain types of equipment, such as hay balers or harvesters. Other mechanics work on equipment that is installed on the farms. For example, *sprinkler-irrigation equipment mechanics* install and maintain self-propelled circle-irrigation systems, which are like giant motorized lawn sprinklers. *Dairy equipment repairers* inspect and repair dairy machinery and equipment such as milking machines, cream separators, and churns.

Most farm equipment mechanics work in the service departments of equipment dealerships. Others are employed by independent repair shops. A smaller number work on large farms that have their own shops.

Requirements

High School

Take technical/shop courses that will introduce you to machinery repair, electrical work, and welding. Mechanical drawing classes can also prepare you for the work. Computer courses will be valuable; computers are used increasingly in farm machinery, as well as in the administrative office of a machine repair and sales business. Science courses that include units in soil and agronomy will help you to understand the needs of the agriculture industry. As a member of the National FFA Organization (formerly the Future Farmers of America), you may be involved in special projects that include working with farm machinery.

Postsecondary Training

After graduating from high school, most farm equipment mechanics go on to complete a one- or two-year program in agricultural or farm mechanics at a vocational school or community college. If you can't find such a program, study in diesel mechanics or appropriate experience through the military are also options. Topics that you will learn about include: the maintenance and repair of diesel and gasoline engines, hydraulic systems, welding, and electronics. Your education doesn't stop there, however. After completing one of these programs you will be hired as a trainee or helper and continue to learn on the job, receiving training from experienced mechanics.

Some farm equipment mechanics learn their trade through apprenticeship programs. These programs combine three to four years of on-the-job training with classroom study related to farm equipment repair and maintenance. Apprentices are usually chosen from among shop helpers.

To stay up-to-date on technological changes that affect their work, mechanics and trainees may take special short-term courses conducted by equipment manufacturers. In these programs, which usually last a few days, company service representatives explain the design and function of new models of equipment and teach mechanics how to maintain and repair them. Some employers help broaden their mechanics' skills by sending them to local vocational schools for special intensive courses in subjects such as air-conditioning repair, hydraulics, or electronics.

Other Requirements

Farm machinery is usually large and heavy. Mechanics need the strength to lift heavy machine parts, such as transmissions. They also need manual dexterity to be able to handle tools and small components. Farm equipment mechanics are usually expected to supply their own hand tools. After years of accumulating favorite tools, experienced mechanics may have collections that represent an investment of thousands of dollars. Employers generally provide all the large power tools and test equipment needed in the shop.

Exploring

Many people who go into farm equipment work have grown up with mechanical repair—they've experimented with lawn mowers, old cars, and other machinery, and they've used a lot of farm equipment. If you don't live on a farm, you may be able to find part-time or summer work on a farm. You can also get valuable mechanical experience working with a gasoline service station, automobile repair shop, or automotive supply house. In addition, consider joining a chapter of the National FFA Organization. This organization is open to students ages 12 to 21 who are enrolled in agricultural programs and offers a wide variety of activities, including career development programs.

Employers

Farm equipment mechanics work in all parts of the country, but there are more job opportunities in the "farm belt"—the Midwestern states. Work is available with independent repair and service businesses, large farm equipment sales companies, and large independent and commercial farms. Some mechanics are self-employed, running their own repair businesses in rural areas. Most independent repair shops employ fewer than five mechanics, while in dealers' service departments there may be 10 or more mechanics on the payroll.

Starting Out

Many people who become trainees in this field have prior experience in related occupations. They may have worked as farmers, farm laborers, heavy-equipment mechanics, automobile mechanics, or air-conditioning mechanics. Although people with this kind of related experience are likely to begin as helpers, their training period may be considerably shorter than the training for beginners with no such experience.

When looking for work, you should apply directly to local farm equipment dealers or independent repair shops. Graduates of vocational schools can often get help finding jobs through their schools' placement service. State employment service offices are another source of job leads, as well as a source of information on any apprenticeships that are available in the region.

Advancement

After they have gained some experience, farm equipment mechanics employed by equipment dealers may be promoted to such positions as shop supervisor, service manager, and eventually manager of the dealership. Some mechanics eventually decide to open their own repair shops (approximately one mechanic in 10 is self-employed). Others become service representatives for farm equipment manufacturers. Additional formal education, such as completion of a two-year associate degree program in agricultural mechanics or a related field, may be required of service representatives.

Earnings

The U.S. Department of Labor reported that in 1998, farm equipment mechanics had median hourly earnings of $10.94. This figure translates into a yearly income of approximately $22,755. In addition, the department reported that the lowest paid mechanics earned about $6.96 per hour ($14,470 per year), while the highest paid earned around $16.01 per hour ($33,300 per year). Exact earnings figures are difficult to determine because farm equipment mechanics do not generally work consistent 40-hour weeks throughout the year. During the busy planting and harvest seasons, for example, mechanics may work many hours of overtime, for which they are usually paid time-and-a-half rates. This overtime pay can substantially increase their weekly earnings. However, during the winter months some mechanics may work less or they may be temporarily laid off, reducing their total income.

Employee benefits may be rare when working for a small shop. A large commercial farm or sales company may offer health insurance plans and sick leave.

Work Environment

Farm equipment mechanics generally work indoors on equipment that has been brought into the shop. Most modern shops are properly ventilated, heated, and lighted. Some older shops may be less comfortable. During harvest seasons, mechanics may have to leave the shop frequently and travel many miles to farms, where they perform emergency repairs outdoors in any kind of weather. They may often work six to seven days a week, 10 to 12 hours a day during this busy season. In the event of an emergency repair, a mechanic often works independently, with little supervision. Mechanics need to be self-reliant and able to solve problems under pressure. When a farm machine breaks down, the lost time can be very expensive for the farmer. A mechanic must be able to diagnose problems quickly and perform repairs without delay.

Grease, gasoline, rust, and dirt are part of the farm equipment mechanic's life. Although safety precautions have improved in recent years, mechanics are often at risk of injury when lifting heavy equipment and parts with jacks or hoists. Other hazards they must routinely guard against include burns from hot engines, cuts from sharp pieces of metal, and exposure to toxic farm chemicals. Following good safety practices can reduce the risks of injury to a minimum.

Outlook

The employment of farm equipment mechanics is expected to decline through 2008 because of the efficiency and dependability of modern farm equipment. To be competitive in the job market, a farm equipment mechanic may need a few years of college training along with some practical experience.

Advancements in technology will soon revolutionize farm equipment. Those working with farm equipment will have to have an understanding of computers, electronics, and highly sophisticated devices and, therefore, a more specialized training. This technology will make farming more efficient and precise. Sensoring devices on planters will be able to determine that all seeds were dropped into the ground; navigation equipment may someday allow the farmer to guide machinery down the row from a remote area. Farm machinery will also be capable of recording the specific needs of a field, determining yield and moisture levels for particular areas.

For More Information

For equipment sales statistics, agricultural reports, and other news of interest to farm mechanics, contact:

Equipment Manufacturers Institute
10 South Riverside Plaza
Chicago, IL 60606-3710
Tel: 312-321-1470
Email: emi@emi.org
Web: http://www.emi.org

Contact FEMA for publications and industry news.

Farm Equipment Manufacturers Association (FEMA)
1000 Executive Parkway, Suite 100
St. Louis, MO 63141-6369
Tel: 314-878-2304
Web: http://www.farmequip.org

Farmers

School Subjects

Business
Earth science

Personal Skills

Leadership/management
Mechanical/manipulative

Work Environment

Primarily outdoors
Primarily multiple locations

Minimum Education Level

High school diploma

Salary Range

$21,000 to $50,000 to $65,000+

Certification or Licensing

Voluntary

Outlook

Decline

Overview

Farmers either own or lease land on which they raise crops such as corn, wheat, tobacco, cotton, vegetables, or fruits; raise animals or poultry, mainly for food; or maintain herds of dairy cattle for the production of milk. Whereas some farmers may combine several of these activities, most specialize in one specific area. They are assisted by farm laborers—either hired workers or members of farm families—who perform various tasks.

As increasingly complex technology continues to impact the agricultural industry, farms are becoming larger. Most contemporary farms are thousands of acres in size and include massive animal and plant production operations. Subsistence farms that produce only enough to support the farmer's family are becoming increasingly rare.

History

In colonial America, almost 95 percent of the population were farmers, planting such crops as corn, wheat, flax, and, further south, tobacco. Livestock including hogs, cattle, sheep, and goats were imported from Europe. Farmers raised hay to feed livestock and just enough other crops to supply their families with a balanced diet throughout the year. Progress in science and technology in the 18th and 19th centuries allowed for societies to develop in different directions, and to build other industries, but over one-half of the world's population is still engaged in farming today.

In the early 20th century, farmers raised a variety of crops along with cattle, poultry, and dairy cows. Farm labor was handled by the farmers and their families. Farmers were very self-sufficient, living on their farms and maintaining their own equipment and storage. Between 1910 and 1960, when horsepower was replaced by mechanized equipment, about 90 million acres previously devoted to growing hay for the feeding of horses could be planted with other crops. Advances in farming techniques and production led to larger farms and more specialization by farmers. Farmers began to focus on growing one or two crops. About this time, more tenant farmers entered the business, renting land for cash or share of the crops.

Farmers doubled their output between 1950 and 1980, but there were fewer of them. In that time, the farm population decreased from 23 million to 6 million. After 1980, farmers began supplementing their household income with off-farm jobs and businesses.

The Job

There are probably as many different types of farmers as there are different types of plants and animals whose products are consumed by humans. In addition to *diversified crops farmers,* who grow different combinations of fruits, grains, and vegetables, and *general farmers*, who raise livestock as well as crops, there are *cash grain farmers*, who grow barley, corn, rice, soybeans, and wheat; vegetable farmers; tree-fruit-and-nut crops farmers; *field crops farmers*, who raise alfalfa, cotton, hops, peanuts, mint, sugarcane, and tobacco; animal breeders; fur farmers; livestock ranchers; dairy farmers; poultry farmers; beekeepers; reptile farmers; fish farmers; and even worm growers.

In addition to the different types of crop farmers, there are two different types of farming management careers: the farm operator and the farm manager.

The *farm operator* either owns his or her own farm or leases land from other farms. Farm operators' responsibilities vary depending on the type of farm they run, but in general they are responsible for making managerial decisions. They determine the best time to seed, fertilize, cultivate, spray, and harvest. They keep extensive financial and inventory records of the farm operations, which are now done with the help of computer programs.

Farm operators perform tasks ranging from caring for livestock to erecting sheds. The size of the farm often determines what tasks the operators handle themselves. On very large farms, operators hire employees to perform tasks that operators on small farms would do themselves.

The *farm manager* has a wide range of duties. The owner of a large livestock farm may hire a farm manager to oversee a single activity, such as feeding the livestock. In other cases, a farm manager may oversee the entire operation of a small farm for an absentee owner. Farm management firms often employ highly skilled farm managers to manage specific operations on a small farm or to oversee tenant farm operations on several farms.

Whether farm operators or managers, the farmers' duties vary widely depending on what product they farm. A common type of farmer is the crop farmer. Following are a number of crops that a crop farmer might manage.

Corn farmers and *wheat farmers* begin the growing season by breaking up the soil with plows, then harrowing, pulverizing, and leveling it. Some of these tasks may be done after the harvest the previous year and others just before planting. Corn is usually planted around the middle of May with machines that place the corn seeds into dirt hills a few inches apart, making weed control easier. On the average, a crop is cultivated three times during a season. Corn is also used in the making of silage, a type of animal feed made by cutting the corn and allowing it to ferment in storage silos.

Wheat may be sown in the fall or spring, depending on the severity of the past winter and the variety of wheat being sown. Wheat is planted with a drill, close together, allowing greater cultivation and easier harvesting. The harvest for winter wheat occurs in early summer. Wheat farmers use combines to gather and thresh the wheat in one operation. The wheat is then stored in large grain storage elevators, which are owned by private individuals, companies, or farming cooperatives.

Cotton and tobacco planting begins in March in the Southwest and somewhat later in the Southeast. Tobacco plants must be carefully protected from harsh weather conditions. The soil in which tobacco is grown must be thoroughly broken up, smoothed, and fertilized before planting, as tobacco is very hard on the soil.

The peanut crop can be managed like other types of farm crops. It is not especially sensitive to weather and disease, nor does it require the great care of tobacco and cotton.

Specialty crops such as fruits and vegetables are subject to seasonal variations, so the farmer usually relies heavily on hired seasonal labor. This type of farmer uses more specialized equipment than do general farmers.

The mechanization of farming has not eliminated all the problems of raising crops. Judgment and experience are always important in making decisions. The *hay farmer*, for example, must determine the time for mowing that will yield the best crop in terms of stem toughness and leaf loss. These decisions must be weighed against possible harsh weather conditions. To harvest hay, hay farmers use specialized equipment such as mowing machines and hay rakes that are usually drawn by tractors. The hay is pressed into bales by another machine for easier storage and then transported to storage facilities or to market.

Decisions about planting are just as crucial as those about harvesting. For example, potatoes need to be planted during a relatively short span of days in the spring. The fields must be tilled and ready for planting, and the farmer must estimate weather conditions so the seedlings will not freeze from late winter weather.

The *crop specialty farmer* uses elaborate irrigation systems to water crops during seasons of inadequate rainfall. Often these systems are portable as it is necessary to move the equipment from field to field.

Farms are strongly influenced by the weather, diseases, fluctuations in prices of domestic and foreign farm products, and, in some cases, federal farm programs. Farmers must carefully plan the combination of crops they will grow so that if the price of one crop drops they will have sufficient income from another to make up for it. Since prices change from month to month, farmers who plan ahead may be able to store their crops or keep their livestock to take advantage of better prices later in the year.

Farmers who raise and breed animals for milk or meat are called *livestock and cattle farmers*. There are various types of farmers that fall into this category.

Livestock farmers generally buy calves from ranchers who breed and raise them. They feed and fatten young cattle and often raise their own corn and hay to lower feeding costs. They need to be familiar with cattle diseases and proper methods of feeding. They provide their cattle with fenced pasturage and adequate shelter from rough weather. Some livestock farmers specialize in breeding stock for sale to ranchers and dairy farmers. These specialists maintain and improve purebred animals of a particular breed. Bulls and cows are then sold to ranchers and dairy farmers who want to improve their herds.

Sheep ranchers raise sheep primarily for their wool. Large herds are maintained on rangeland in the western states. Since large areas of land are needed, the sheep rancher must usually buy grazing rights on government-owned lands.

Although the first concern of *dairy farmers* is the production of high-grade milk, they also raise corn and grain to provide feed for their animals. Dairy farmers must be able to repair the many kinds of equipment essential to their business and know about diseases, sanitation, and methods of improving the quantity and quality of the milk.

Dairy animals must be milked twice every day, once in the morning and once at night. Records are kept of each cow's production of milk to ascertain which cows are profitable and which should be traded or sold for meat. After milking, when the cows are at pasture, the farmer cleans the stalls and barn by washing, sweeping, and sterilizing milking equipment with boiling water. This is extremely important because dairy cows easily contract diseases from unsanitary conditions, and this in turn may contaminate the milk. Dairy farmers must have their herds certified to be free of disease by the U.S. Department of Health.

The great majority of *poultry farmers* do not hatch their own chicks but buy them from commercial hatcheries. The chicks are kept in brooder houses until they are seven or eight weeks old and are then transferred to open pens or shelters. After six months, the hens begin to lay eggs and roosters are culled from the flock to be sold for meat.

The primary duty of poultry farmers is to keep their flocks healthy. They provide shelter from the chickens' natural enemies and from extreme weather conditions. The shelters are kept extremely clean, because diseases can spread through a flock rapidly. The poultry farmer selects the food that best allows each chicken to grow or produce to its greatest potential while at the same time keeping costs down.

Raising chickens to be sold as broilers or fryers requires equipment to house them until they are six to 13 weeks old. Farmers specializing in the production of eggs gather eggs at least twice a day and more often in very warm weather. The eggs then are stored in a cool place, inspected, graded, and packed for market. The poultry farmer who specializes in producing broilers is usually not an independent producer but is under contract with a backer, who is often the operator of a slaughterhouse or the manufacturer of poultry feeds.

Beekeepers set up and manage bee hives and harvest and sell the excess honey that bees don't use as their own food. The sale of honey is less profitable than the business of cultivating bees for lease to farmers to help pollinate their crops.

Farmers and farm managers make a wide range of administrative decisions. In addition to their knowledge of crop production and animal science, they determine how to market the foods they produce. They keep an eye on the commodities markets to see which crops are most profitable. They take out loans to buy farm equipment or additional land for cultivation. They keep up with new methods of production and new markets. Farms today are large, complex businesses, complete with the requisite anxiety over cash flow, competition, markets, and production.

Requirements

High School

Take classes in math, accounting, and business to prepare for the management responsibilities of running a farm. To further assist you in management, take computer classes. Chemistry, biology, and earth science classes can help you understand the various processes of crop production. Technical and shop courses will help you to better understand agricultural machinery. With county extension courses, you can keep abreast of developments in farm technology.

Postsecondary Training

Although there are no specific educational requirements for this field, every successful farmer, whether working with crops or animals, must have a knowledge of the principles of soil preparation and cultivation, disease control, and machinery maintenance, as well as a mastery of business practices and bookkeeping. Farmers must know their crops well enough to be able to choose the proper seeds for their particular soil and climate. They also need experience in evaluating crop growth and weather cycles. Livestock and dairy farmers should enjoy working with animals and have some background in animal science, breeding, and care.

The state land-grant universities across the country were established to encourage agricultural research and to educate young people in the latest advancements in farming. They offer agricultural programs that award bachelor's degrees as well as shorter programs in specific areas. Some universities offer advanced studies in horticulture, animal science, agronomy, and agricultural economics. Most students in agricultural colleges are also required to take courses in farm management, business, finance, and economics. Two-year colleges often have programs leading to associate degrees in agriculture.

Certification or Licensing

The American Society of Farm Managers and Rural Appraisers offers farm operators voluntary certification as an accredited farm manager. Certification requires several years experience working on a farm, an academic background—a bachelor's or preferably a master's degree in a branch of agricultural science—and courses covering the business, financial, and legal aspects of farm management.

Other Requirements

You'll need to keep up to date on new farming methods throughout the world. You must be flexible and innovative enough to adapt to new technologies that will produce crops or raise livestock more efficiently. You should also have good mechanical aptitude and be able to work with a wide variety of tools and machinery.

Exploring

Most people who become farmers have grown up on farms; if your family doesn't own a farm, there are opportunities for part-time work as a hired hand, especially during seasonal operations. If you live in an agricultural community, you should be able to find work as a detasseler in the summer time. Although the work is hot and strenuous, it will quickly familiarize you with aspects of crop production and the hard work it takes to operate a farm.

In addition, organizations such as 4-H and the National FFA Organization (formerly Future Farmers of America) offer good opportunities for learning about, visiting, and participating in farming activities. Agricultural colleges often have their own farms where students can gain actual experience in farm operations in addition to classroom work.

Employers

Farmers are self-employed, working on land they've inherited, purchased, or leased. Those who don't own land, but who have farming experience, may find work on large commercial farms or with agricultural supply companies as consultants or managers. Farmers with seasonal crops may work for agriculture-related businesses during the off-season or may work temporarily as farm hands for livestock farms and ranches. They may also own other businesses, such as farm equipment sales and service.

Starting Out

It is becoming increasingly difficult for a person to purchase land for farming. The capital investment in a farm today is so great that it is almost impossible for anyone to start from scratch. However, those who lack a family connection to farming or who do not have enough money to start their own farm can lease land from other farmers. Money for leasing land and equipment may be available from local banks or the Farmers Home Administration.

Because the capital outlay is so high, many wheat, corn, and specialty crop farmers often start as tenant farmers, renting land and equipment. They may also share the cash profits with the owner of the land. In this way, these tenants hope to gain both the experience and cash to purchase and manage their own farms.

Livestock farmers generally start by renting property and sometimes animals on a share-of-the-profits basis with the owner. Government lands, such as national parks, can be rented for pasture as well. Later, when the livestock farmer wants to own property, it is possible to borrow based on the estimated value of the leased land, buildings, and animals. Dairy farmers can begin in much the same way. However, loans are becoming more difficult to obtain. After several years of lenient loan policies, financial institutions in farm regions have tightened their requirements.

Advancement

Farmers advance by buying their own farms or additional acreage to increase production and income. With a farm's success, a farmer can also invest in better equipment and technology and can hire managers and workers to attend to much of the farm's operation. This is true for crop, livestock, dairy, or poultry farmers. In farming, as in other fields, a person's success depends greatly on education, motivation, and keeping up with the latest developments.

Earnings

Farmers' incomes vary greatly from year to year, since the prices of farm products fluctuate according to weather conditions and the amount and quality of what all farmers were able to produce. A farm that shows a large profit one year may show a loss for the following year. Many farmers, especially small ones, earn incomes from nonfarm activities that are several times larger than their farm incomes.

Farm incomes also vary greatly depending on the size and type of farm. In general, large farms generate more income than small farms. Exceptions include some specialty farms that produce low-volume but high-quality horticultural and fruit products.

In 1998, the U.S. Department of Agriculture (USDA) projected the net income for the country's two million farms to be $42.5 billion. This was a decline from 1997's $49.9 billion and 1996's $53.5 billion. The 1998 figure averages out to $21,250 per farm. The 1998 *USDA Agriculture Fact Book* includes results from a recent survey that found that the average farm household income was $50,360, which includes income from off-farm jobs and businesses. The same survey showed that 6 percent of the farmers had negative household incomes.

Work Environment

The farmer's daily life has its rewards and dangers. Machine-related injuries, exposure to the weather, and illnesses caused by allergies or animal-related diseases are just some of the hazards that farmers face on a regular basis. In addition, farms are often isolated, away from many conveniences and necessities such as immediate medical attention.

Farming can be a difficult and frustrating career, but for many it is a satisfying way of life. The hours are long and the work is physically strenuous, but working outdoors and watching the fruits of one's labor grow before one's eyes can be very rewarding. The changing seasons bring variety to the day-to-day work. Farmers seldom work five eight-hour days a week. When harvesting time comes or the weather is right for planting or spraying, farmers work long hours to see that everything gets done. Even during the cold winter months they stay busy repairing machinery and buildings. Dairy farmers and other livestock farmers work seven days a week all year round.

Outlook

The *Occupational Outlook Handbook* reports that there were nearly 1.5 million farmers and farm managers in 1998. Every year can be different for farmers, as production, expansion, and markets are affected by weather, exports, and other factors. Land prices are expected to drop some, but so are the prices for grain, hogs, and cattle. Throughout the 20th century, the U.S. government was active in aiding farmers, but in recent years has attempted to step back from agricultural production. But the state of farming today is calling for more government involvement. Some trends that farmers may follow in their efforts to increase income include more diversified crop production; for example, farmers may choose to plant high-oil or high-protein corn, which bring more money in the marketplace. But these new grains also require different methods of storage and marketing.

Large corporate farms are fast replacing the small farmer, who is being forced out of the industry by the spiraling costs of feed, grain, land, and equipment. The late 1970s and early 1980s were an especially hard time for farmers. Many small farmers were forced to give up farming; some lost farms that had been in their families for generations. Some small-scale farmers, however, have found opportunities in organic food production, farmers' markets, and similar market niches that require more direct personal contact with their customers.

Despite the great difficulty in becoming a farmer today, there are many agriculture-related careers that involve people with farm production, marketing, management, and agribusiness. Those with an interest in farming will likely have to pursue these alternative career paths.

For More Information

The Farm Bureau hosts youth conferences and other events for those interested in farming; its Web page includes articles of interest to farmers.

American Farm Bureau Federation
225 Touhy Avenue
Park Ridge, IL 60068
Tel: 847-685-8600
Web: http://www.fb.org

For more information on the farming industry, contact the following organizations:

4-H
Stop 2225
1400 Independence Avenue, SW
Washington, DC 20250-2225
Tel: 202-720-2908
Web: http://www.4h-usa.org

National Council of Farmer Cooperatives
50 F Street, NW, Suite 900
Washington, DC 20001
Tel: 202-626-8700
Web: http://www.ncfc.org

National FFA Organization
6060 FFA Drive
PO Box 68960
Indianapolis, IN 46268
Tel: 317-802-6060
Web: http://www.ffa.org

U.S. Department of Agriculture
Higher Education Program
14th Street and Independence, SW
Washington, DC 20250
Tel: 202-720-2791
Web: http://www.usda.gov

Food Technologists

Chemistry Mathematics	School Subjects
Following instructions Technical/scientific	Personal Skills
Primarily indoors Primarily one location	Work Environment
Bachelor's degree	Minimum Education Level
$20,000 to $51,000 to $100,000	Salary Range
Voluntary	Certification or Licensing
About as fast as the average	Outlook

Overview

Food technologists, sometimes known as *food scientists*, study the physical, chemical, and biological composition of food. They develop methods for safely processing, preserving, and packaging food and search for ways to improve its flavor and nutritional value. They also conduct tests to ensure that products, from fresh produce to packaged meals, meet industry and government standards.

History

One of the earliest methods of food preservation was drying. Grains were sun- and air-dried to prevent mold growth and insect damage. Fruits and vegetables dried in the sun and meats dried and smoked over a fire were stored for use during times of need. Fruits were preserved by fermenting them into wines and vinegars, and fermented milk became curds, cheeses, and yogurts.

Methods of food preservation improved over the centuries, but there were severe limitations until the evolution of scientific methods made it possible to preserve food. By creating conditions unfavorable to the growth or survival of spoilage microorganisms and preventing deterioration by enzymes, scientists were able to extend the storage life of foods well beyond the normal period.

For most of history, people bought or traded for bulk foods, such as grain or rice, rather than prepared foods. This began to change in the early 1800s, when new methods of preserving and packaging foods were developed. The science of food technology did not, however, really develop until shortly before the American entrance into World War II. Prompted by the need to supply U.S. troops with nutritious, flavorful foods that were not only easy to transport but also kept for long periods of time, scientists around 1940 began making great advances in the preparation, preservation, and packaging of foods. By the 1950s, food science and food technology departments were being established by many universities, and food science disciplines became important and respected areas of study.

Another boost to the food technology program came with the U.S. space program; new types of foods, as well as new types of preparation, packaging, and processing were needed to feed astronauts in space.

By the late 20th century, few people still canned or preserved their own fruits and vegetables. Advances in production methods in this century have made it possible to process larger quantities of a wider range of food products. Scientists specializing in food technology have found better ways to retard spoilage, improve flavor, and provide foods that are consistent in quality, flavor, texture, and size. Innovations such as freeze drying, irradiation, and artificial coloring and flavoring have changed the way many of the foods we eat are processed and prepared. Consumer demand for an ever-increasing variety of foods has created a demand for food technologists to develop them. Foods processed in a variety of ways are readily available to the consumer and have become such an accepted part of modern life that one rarely gives a thought to the complexities involved. The safety of the process, nutrition, development of new products and production methods, and the packaging of products are all the responsibility of food technologists.

The Job

Food technologists usually specialize in one phase of food technology. About one-third are involved in research and development. A large number are employed in quality-control laboratories or in the production or processing areas of food plants. Others teach or perform basic research in colleges and universities, work in sales or management positions, or are employed as technical writers or consultants. The branches of food technology are numerous and include cereal grains, meat and poultry, fats and oils, seafood, animal foods, beverages, dairy products, flavors, sugar and starches, stabilizers, preservatives, colors, and nutritional additives.

Food technologists in basic research study the structure and composition of food and observe the changes that take place during storage or processing. The knowledge they gain may enable them to develop new sources of proteins, determine the effects of processing on microorganisms, or isolate factors that affect the flavor, appearance, or texture of foods. Technologists engaged in applied research and development have the more practical task of creating new food products and developing new processing methods. They also continue to work with existing foods to make them more nutritious and flavorful and to improve their color and texture.

A rapidly growing area of food technology is biotechnology. Food technologists in this area work with plant breeding, gene splicing, microbial fermentation, and plant cell tissue cultures to produce enhanced raw products for processing.

Foods may lose their characteristics and nutritious value during processing and storage. Food technologists seek ways to prevent this by developing improved methods for processing, production, quality control, packaging, and distribution. They conduct chemical and microbiological tests on products to be sure they conform to standards set by the government and by the food industry. They also determine the nutritive content (the amounts of sugar, starch, protein, fat, vitamins, and minerals) that federal regulations say must be printed on the labels.

Food technologists in quality-control laboratories concentrate on ensuring that foods in every stage of processing meet industry and government standards. They check to see that raw ingredients are fresh, sufficiently ripe, and suitable for processing. They conduct periodic inspections of processing line operations. They also test after processing to be sure that various enzymes are not active and that bacteria levels are low enough so the food will not spoil or be unsafe to eat.

Some technologists test new products in test kitchens or develop new processing methods in laboratory pilot plants. Others devise new methods for packaging and storing foods. To solve problems, they may confer with processing engineers, flavor experts, or packaging and marketing specialists.

In processing plants, food technologists are responsible for preparing production specifications and scheduling processing operations. They ensure that proper temperature and humidity levels are maintained in storage areas and that wastes are disposed of properly and other sanitary regulations are observed throughout the plant. They also make recommendations to management in matters relating to efficiency or economy, such as new equipment or suppliers.

Some food technologists have positions in other fields where they can apply their specialized knowledge to such areas as advertising, market research, or technical sales.

Requirements

High School

Students in high school can prepare for a technologist career by taking courses in biology, chemistry, physics, and mathematics, along with other college-preparatory courses.

Postsecondary Training

Educational requirements for this field are high. Beginners need at least a bachelor's degree in food technology. Some technologists hold degrees in other areas, such as chemistry, biology, engineering, agriculture, or business, and nearly half have advanced degrees. Master's degrees and doctorates are mandatory for college teaching and are usually necessary for management and research positions.

Undergraduate programs in food technology are offered by approximately 60 colleges and universities. Of these, 45 have been approved by the Institute of Food Technologists. Courses include physics, biochemistry, mathematics, microbiology, the social sciences and humanities, and business administration, in addition to food technology courses such as food preservation, processing, sanitation, and marketing. Most of these schools also offer advanced degrees, usually in specialized areas of food technology. To successfully complete their program, candidates for a master's degree or a doctoral degree must perform extensive research and write a thesis reporting their original findings. Specialists in administrative, managerial, or regulatory areas may earn advanced degrees in business administration or in law rather than in food technology.

Other Requirements

Food technologists should have analytical minds and enjoy technical work. In addition, they must be able to express themselves clearly and be detail oriented. They also must be able to work well in group situations and participate and contribute to a team effort.

Exploring

Students may be able to arrange field trips to local food processing plants and plan interviews with or lectures by experts in the field. Apart from an interest in science, and especially chemistry, the prospective food technologist may also develop an interest in cooking and in inventing their own recipes.

Because of the educational requirements for food technologists, it is not likely that students will be able to acquire actual experience while still in high school. Part-time and summer employment as workers in food processing plants, however, would provide an excellent overview of the industry. More advanced college students may have opportunities for jobs helping out in research laboratories.

Employers

Food technologists work in a wide variety of settings, including food processing plants, food ingredient plants, and food manufacturing plants. They may work in basic research, product development, processing and quality assurance, packaging, or market research. There are positions in laboratories, test kitchens, and on production lines as well as with government agencies.

Starting Out

Many schools offering degree programs in food science will also offer job placement assistance. Also, recruiters from private industry frequently conduct interviews on campus. Faculty members may be willing to grant referrals to exceptional students. Another method is to make direct application to individual companies.

Frequently, the food products with which food technologists work determine where they are employed. Those who work with meats or grains may work in the Midwest. Technologists who work with citrus fruits usually work in Florida or California. Two-thirds of all food technologists are employed by private industry. The remaining work for the federal government. Some major government employers of food technologists include the Environmental Protection Agency, National Aeronautics and Space Administration, the Food and Drug Administration, and the United States Department of Agriculture.

Advancement

For food technologists with a bachelor's degree, there are two general paths to advancement, depending on whether they work in production or in research. They may begin as *quality-assurance chemists* or *assistant production managers* and, with experience, move up to more responsible management positions. Some technologists may start as *junior food chemists* in the research and development laboratory of a food company and advance to section head or another research management position.

Technologists who hold master's degrees may start out as *food chemists* in a research and development laboratory. Those with doctorates usually begin their careers in basic research or teaching. Other food technologists may gain expertise in more specialized areas and become *sensory evaluation experts* or *food marketing specialists*.

Earnings

According to the Institute of Food Technologists, in 1997 salaries for food technologists ranged from $19,200 to $200,000. The overall median salary was $60,000. According to the *Occupational Outlook Handbook*, median annual earnings of agricultural and food scientists were $42,340 in 1998.

Beginning food technologists with a bachelor's degree in food science or a related discipline average about $29,300 per year. With experience, food technologists earn about $47,000 per year. Those with advanced degrees can earn considerably more. The average salary for food technologists holding a master's degree in science is about $51,000 per year. Food technologists with doctoral degrees earn over $65,000 per year, while those with an MBA degree can earn $75,000 per year or more.

Food technologists with a bachelor's degree who work for the federal government earn starting salaries that range from $19,700 to $26,700 a year. After several years of employment, government food technologists may earn between $35,000 and $50,000 a year.

Food technologist salaries vary somewhat depending on the region where they work. Those in the South Atlantic and Pacific states generally earn the highest salaries, while those in the West South Central states of Texas, Oklahoma, Arkansas, and Louisiana earn the lowest salaries. However, the cost of living in a particular area plays a role in the level of a food technologist's salary.

Most food technologists will receive generous benefit plans, which usually include health insurance, life insurance, pension plans, and vacation and sick pay. Others may receive funds for continuing education.

Work Environment

Most food technologists work regular hours in clean, well-lighted, temperature-controlled offices, laboratories, or classrooms. Technologists in production and quality-control work in processing plants may be subject to machine noise and hot or cold conditions.

Outlook

The food industry is the largest single industry in the United States and throughout the world. There are roughly 70,000 food technologists employed in the United States. Because people have to eat, there will always be a need for people to develop, test, and process food products. In developed countries, the ever-present consumer demand for new and different food products means that the outlook for food scientists and technologists is very good.

Several factors have also increased the demand for skilled technologists. New labeling laws enacted in the 1990s have required companies to provide detailed nutritional information on their products. The continuing trend toward more healthful eating habits has recently focused on the roles of fats, cholesterol, and salt in nutrition, and companies have rushed to create a variety of low-fat, low-sodium, fat-free, cholesterol-free, and sodium-free foods. A larger and more varied supply of wholesome and economical food is needed to satisfy current tastes. The food industry will have to produce convenience foods of greater quality for use in homes and for the food service institutions that supply airlines, restaurants, and other major customers. More technologists may be hired to research and produce new foods from modifications of wheat, corn, rice, and soybeans, such as the "meat" products made from vegetable proteins. The food industry has increased its spending in recent years for this kind of research and development and is likely to continue to do so. Developing these products, without sacrificing such important factors as taste, appearance, and texture, has produced many new opportunities for food technologists.

Food technologists will also be sought to produce new foods for poor and starving people in underdeveloped countries. Experienced technologists will use their advanced training to create new foods from such "staples" as rice, corn, wheat, and soybeans.

Finally, the increasing emphasis on the automation of many elements of food processing has also created a need for food technologists to adapt cooking and preparation processes to the new technology.

For More Information

For information on accredited educational programs in food science, contact:

Institute of Food Technologists
221 North LaSalle Street, Suite 300
Chicago, IL 60601-1291
Tel: 312-782-8424
Web: http://www.ift.org/

National Food Processors Association
1350 I Street, NW, Suite 300
Washington, DC 20005
Tel: 202-639-5900
Web: http://www.nfpa-food.org

U.S. Department of Agriculture
14th Street and Independence Avenue, SW
Washington, DC 20250
Web: http://www.usda.gov/

Grain Merchants

School Subjects

Business
Mathematics

Personal Skills

Leadership/management
Mechanical/manipulative

Work Environment

Primarily indoors
Primarily multiple locations

Minimum Education Level

Bachelor's degree

Salary Range

$18,000 to $31,564 to $50,000

Certification or Licensing

Required for certain positions

Outlook

About as fast as the average

Overview

Grain merchants buy grain from farms and sell it to consumers. Between the buying and the selling, they are concerned with the quality, market value, shipping, processing, and storing of the grain. In effect, they are liaisons between the farmer and the eventual user or consumer of the grain. The regulation activities of the grain merchant create an efficient market for grain around the world. Grain merchants work as either grain buyers or grain managers.

History

Trading grain in the past was relatively simple. Farmers sold their wheat, corn, oats, barley, and rice in the public market in their town. People bought enough grain to meet their families' needs, and farmers purchased grain for their animals. As grain production grew, firms that purchased, stored, processed, and transported grains were established. In certain cities with good transportation facilities, such as Chicago and Kansas City, grain exchanges where grain merchants could buy and sell their commodities were established.

Today the buying and selling of grain is a complicated process involving farmers, merchants, food processors, and consumers. Grain merchants have played a vital role in making this process more efficient. Farmers, unlike factories, can only harvest their crops when they are ripe, but consumers need their produce all year round. By purchasing, processing, transporting, and storing grain until other buyers can be found, grain merchants facilitate the smooth flow of the commodity all year round, during times of both shortages and surpluses. This results in a fair market price for the farmer and a steady supply of food for the consumer.

The Job

Grain elevators are structures that resemble silos where grain is stored and sold. They are a common sight in the agricultural and livestock regions of the Midwest, South, and Southwest. Grain merchants do most of their buying at the local grain elevator, where they meet with area farmers and try to negotiate a fair price. The grain elevator, which may be privately or cooperatively owned, then sells its grain to the terminal elevators located in cities with good transportation access, such as Chicago, Minneapolis, Omaha, Kansas City, and Fort Worth.

Grain merchants must have good instincts about when it will be most profitable to purchase grain. They may buy grain when the supply they have on hand reaches a predetermined reorder point, when a person or company specially orders it, or when market conditions are especially favorable. When purchasing grain, merchants must consider the type of grain specified, its market price, quantity discounts, freight handling or other transportation costs, and delivery time. Much of this information can be obtained by comparing listings in catalogs and trade journals, interviewing suppliers' representatives, keeping up with current market trends, and examining samples. Many grain merchants are dependent on computers for online access to up-to-date price listings or programs that keep track of inventory levels and process routine orders.

Merchants must be sufficiently familiar with the various qualities of grain to determine whether to purchase certain grains. They inspect samples of grain by weighing them, checking their moisture content, and examining them for insects or other damage. Grain must also be classified according to type. The U.S. Department of Agriculture (USDA) has developed grain standards to ensure that grains of a certain grade from all over the country meet the same specifications. After merchants make an initial appraisal of the quality of the grain, they send samples to a federal *grain inspector* for an official appraisal. Although grain merchants often are involved in many aspects of the buying, storing, and reselling process, there are two major specialists who perform different functions in this occupation.

Grain buyers evaluate and purchase grain for resale and milling. They select the type of grain to order based on current demand and possible future considerations. Grain buyers arrange for the transportation and storage of the grain and identify possible resale markets. They hope to make money by reselling the grain for a higher price than they paid for it. They either buy the grain themselves, hoping to sell it in the near future, or buy and sell for businesses, making a commission on each sale.

Buyers must keep up-to-date on all information that affects grain and grain prices. In making purchasing decisions they must take into account the weather, planting schedules, consumer trends, crop qualities, and government standards both in the United States and abroad.

Because of market fluctuations in the price of grains, holding on to grain for any length of time is risky. To minimize their risk, buyers may purchase commodity futures, which are agreements to buy or sell an amount of grain at a future date. These futures are hedges against changes in the price of grain. Later the buyers sell their supply of grain to a food processor or grain exporter and buy back their hedges.

Grain managers work at terminal elevators or other holding facilities. Managers must inspect all the grain that comes to the holding terminal and calculate its market value. In estimating its market value, managers look at moisture content, protein, oil, damage, and the presence of live insects, as well as costs for transportation and handling. They may also send samples to federal grain inspection agencies for a government standardized analysis.

Managers keep daily records on the kinds and grades of grain received, prices paid, amount purchased, and the amount in storage. They also supervise grain elevator workers in the unloading, loading, storing, and mixing of the grain for shipment and milling.

Requirements

High School

You should take classes in business, accounting, history, and economics, to get a sense of world markets and trading. English and composition courses will help you develop communication skills needed for working with farmers, managers, and other agribusiness professionals. Mathematics classes will help you prepare for the accounting, calculating, and analysis involved in this work. If your high school offers courses in agriculture, take those that will teach you about crop production. Other classes that will give you an understanding of plant growth and the environment include earth sciences, biology, and chemistry.

Postsecondary Training

Though you may be able to get some assistant positions with only a high school diploma, many grain merchants have undergraduate or graduate degrees in agriculture, economics, or business management from a college or university. However, two-year programs can also be beneficial. In either case, the prospective grain merchant should take courses in agricultural economics, accounting, purchasing, finance, and business law. As finances in the agricultural sector tighten and some farmers go out of business, future grain merchants will probably deal with fewer, more specialized farms.

Certification or Licensing

Grain merchants in commodity futures, who deal directly with the public, must be licensed by the federal government. They must also meet a code of ethics and a series of guidelines set up to test their skills.

Other Requirements

In order to be successful, you must have an excellent rapport with farmers and other suppliers. This relationship determines whether you'll be able to get a good price on the grain, favorable payment terms, quick delivery on emergency orders, or help in obtaining the grain during times of scarcity. To negotiate these and other conditions, you must have good communications skills, be able to work effectively with others, and handle high-pressure situations. You must be persuasive, diplomatic, and cooperative. As with most business jobs, one gets ahead with initiative, dependability, good judgment, and trustworthiness.

Exploring

If you live in an agricultural community with grain elevators, you might be able to find part-time or seasonal work with a farming cooperative or other grain purchasing organization. It may also be possible to get part-time work at a commodities exchange to learn about the profession from that angle. In addition, some school work-study programs provide opportunities for part-time, on-the-job training with grain elevators. Also, consider joining your school's branch of the National FFA Organization (formerly Future Farmers of America) to learn more about the role of agriculture in today's society.

Employers

Grain merchants may work in local grain elevators in agricultural communities or with the corporate headquarters of major grain companies. They also find work in commodities exchanges. Companies that supply products and equipment to grain processing companies hire people with elevator management and agribusiness experience. USDA and other government agencies also hire grain merchants; the USDA Grain Inspection, Packers, and Stockyards Administration sponsors many projects that require grain professionals.

Starting Out

A good college program will include internship opportunities, as well as career placement services. Jobs with grain elevators will be advertised in the newspaper; entry level positions include grain elevator worker and commodities exchange clerk. With some experience, you can move into an assistant manager or assistant operator position. The Grain Elevator and Processing Society serves as the professional organization for grain professionals and sponsors annual conventions and other opportunities for members to network with others in the industry.

Advancement

A skilled grain merchant may become a grain elevator manager or a grain buyer for a large company. As always, those with the most training and experience stand the best prospects of advancing to positions of higher pay and greater responsibility. Changing employers is another way to advance in this field. Some skilled grain merchants become consultants for the federal government or take a similar position with a bank, insurance company, or other private company.

Earnings

As with other brokers, some grain merchants work on a commission basis and others work for a straight salary. Earnings vary depending on the size of the employer, the experience of the employee, and the specific job responsibilities. Beginning grain merchants can expect to earn $18,000 to $26,000 per year. Experienced grain merchants earn between an average of $39,000 and $50,000 annually. The mean yearly income for all farm products purchasing agents and buyers (including grain merchants) was $31,564 according to the 1998 edition of the *O*Net Dictionary of Occupational Titles*. Salaries, overall, are highest for elevator managers at large regional terminals and for successful grain buyers and brokers. While grain brokers and commodities traders can earn quite a bit of money, the nature of their work means they could lose huge amounts as well. A great deal of a grain merchant's success depends on making the proper contacts with grain suppliers and buyers. Those who work for the federal government may earn somewhat less than those in the private sector. Full-time grain merchants usually receive paid holidays, health insurance, and other benefits. Many firms also have pension plans.

Work Environment

The work environment of a grain merchant can vary from a typical office setting to the drama of a trading room floor. It is a profession that often requires taking great risks and as a result, receiving great rewards or great disappointment.

Grain merchants generally work a standard week of 37 to 40 hours, although overtime is likely in situations when grain supplies are in demand or in a state of flux. Some grain merchants, especially grain buyers, travel a great deal. These trips are necessary to buy and sell grain, make any necessary inspections, and keep in contact with current and prospective clients. Those who travel are usually reimbursed for expenses incurred for lodging, transportation, and other necessities.

Outlook

The populations of small agricultural communities are rapidly decreasing in some parts of the country, particularly in the plains states. Though many of the grain elevators are closing in these areas as farmers look for more stable sources of income, grain is still in great demand around the world. Agribusiness professionals, consultants, and the U.S. government are all involved in increasing this demand by searching for new, efficient uses for grain. Scientific advances will also aid in the storage and processing of grain.

A number of issues affect the grain industry every year, and results are often difficult to predict. Grain production and sales are influenced by weather, planting seasons, and the overseas market. In addition, the technological development of genetically modified grains has lead to increased production but also resulted in grain products that are impossible to sell in some markets. The railroad industry can also affect grain sales—if there aren't enough rail cars available to haul the grain away, elevators with limited storage and excess grain are forced to pile the grain on the ground. Decisions by government agencies such as the USDA and the Environmental Protection Agency also determine the way grain merchants do business. Laws concerning emissions standards and storage facilities sometimes call for costly repairs and down time.

For More Information

To learn about various programs and the government's role in the marketing of grain, contact:

USDA Grain Inspection, Packers, and Stockyards Administration
PO Box 96454
Washington DC 20090
Tel: 202-720-5091
Web: http://www.usda.gov/agency/gipsa

Health and Regulatory Inspectors

School Subjects

Biology
Health

Personal Skills

Communication/ideas
Technical/scientific

Work Environment

Indoors and outdoors
Primarily multiple locations

Minimum Education Level

Bachelor's degree

Salary Range

$25,500 to $35,200 to $54,000+

Certification or Licensing

Required for certain positions

Outlook

About as fast as the average

Overview

Health and regulatory inspectors are employed by the federal, state, or local governments to enforce those laws that protect public health and safety, as well as certain regulatory laws that govern, for example, transportation, food processing, and waste disposal.

History

Federal, state, and local laws have been enacted to provide service and protection to citizens in many areas of daily life. An important aspect of law enforcement involves setting acceptable standards in such diverse areas as quality of transportation and food storage and then providing ways to ensure that these standards are met. Government takes responsibility for public safety on many fronts, including as it relates to the agricultural industry. Over the years, federal, state, and local governments have developed a system of regular inspection and reporting to ensure that these safety standards are maintained.

Rather than wait until a law has been violated, it is more efficient to employ inspectors to watch continuously the way in which standards requirements are carried out. For example, if a law requires that food be stored at a certain temperature to prevent the growth of microorganisms, regular inspections of the place where the food is stored ensure the law is followed, which is better than waiting until disease or illness occurs. Health and regulatory inspectors ensure compliance with all health and safety laws and regulations.

A myriad of local, state, and federal agencies oversee the vast areas of inspection and regulation that are required in such a large nation. One major employer is the U.S. Department of Health and Human Services. This department was formed in 1953 as a successor to the Federal Security Agency, which had been set up in 1939 to "administer federal responsibilities in the field of health, education, and social security." In 1979 the department was organized into five main operating components, one of which, the Public Health Service (serving the nation since 1798), operates numerous health and regulatory subagencies including the Food and Drug Administration, the National Institutes of Health, and the Federal Aviation Administration. Other employers of health and regulatory inspectors include the Environmental Protection Agency, the Department of the Interior, the Department of Agriculture, the Occupational Safety and Health Administration, and many others on the federal, state, and local levels.

The Job

Since there are so many areas that require regulation, there are different types of specialists within the field of health and regulatory inspection who determine how compliance with laws can best be met. The following is a list of some of the major kinds of food-related inspectors employed by the government:

Food and drug inspectors check firms that produce, store, handle, and market food, drugs, and cosmetics. Packaging must be accurately labeled to list contents, and inspectors perform spot checks to confirm this. The weight or measurement of a product must also be accurate. The inspectors use scales, thermometers, chemical testing kits, container-sampling devices, ultraviolet lights, and cameras to test various substances. They look for bacteriological or chemical contamination and assemble evidence if a product is harmful to the public health or does not meet other standards.

Food inspectors are empowered by state and federal law to inspect meat, poultry, and their by-products to ensure these are safe for public consumption. In a slaughterhouse the inspection team leader is always a veterinarian who can ensure that the animals are healthy. Proper sanitation, processing, packaging, and labeling are constantly inspected. Specialists concerned with raising animals for consumption and with processing meat and meat products include *veterinary livestock inspectors*, *veterinary virus-serum inspectors*, and *veterinary meat inspectors*.

Agricultural chemicals inspectors inspect establishments where agricultural service products—such as fertilizers, pesticides, and livestock feed and medications—are manufactured, marketed, and used. They may monitor distribution warehouses, retail outlets, processing plants, and private and industrial farms to collect samples of their products for analysis. If there is a violation, they gather information and samples for use as legal evidence.

Agricultural commodity graders ensure that retailers and consumers get reliable and safe commodities. They may specialize in cotton, dairy products, eggs and egg products, grains, or processed or fresh fruit or vegetables. For example, eggs must meet size and weight standards; dairy products must meet the standards set for butterfat content; and other products must meet standards of cleanliness and quality. The inspectors check product standards and issue official grading certificates. They also ensure sanitation standards by means of regular inspection of plants and equipment.

Agricultural quarantine inspectors work to protect crops, forests, gardens, and livestock from the introduction and spread of plant pests and animal diseases. They inspect aircraft, ships, railway cars, and other transportation entering the United States for restricted or prohibited plant or animal materials. They also work to prevent the spread of agricultural disease from one state or one part of the country to another.

Agricultural-chemical registration specialists review and evaluate information on pesticides, fertilizers, and other products containing dangerous chemicals. If the manufacturers or distributors of the products have complied with government regulations, their applications for registration are approved.

Environmental health inspectors, also called *sanitarians*, work primarily for state and local governments to ensure that government standards of cleanliness and purity are met in food, water, and air. They may inspect processing plants, dairies, restaurants, hospitals, and other institutions. This involves the inspection of handling, processing, and serving of food and of the treatment and disposal of garbage, sewage, and refuse.

Finding the nature and cause of pollution means inspecting those places where pollution might occur, testing for pollutants, and collecting samples of air, water, waste, and soil for analysis. The environmental health inspector initiates action to stop pollution and is vigilant to ensure that offenses are not repeated. In urban situations the environmental health inspector may specialize in just one area such as industrial waste inspection, water-pollution control, or pesticide control.

Environmental health inspectors in state or local agricultural or health departments may specialize in milk and dairy production, water or air pollution, food or institutional sanitation, or occupational health.

Health inspectors may travel to a variety of sites such as restaurants and hospitals. The health inspectors in a processing plant generally work solely at that site, and the same may be true of dairy product inspectors and sewage processing plant inspectors. The work involves making reports to the government regulatory agency for which the inspector works, as well as to the management of the institution or company being inspected.

Occupational safety and health inspectors enforce the regulations of the Occupational Safety and Health Administration and of state and local governments. They are also employed in the private sector, where they have similar responsibilities. Their duties include inspecting machinery, working conditions, and equipment to ensure that proper safety precautions are used that meet government standards and regulations.

Safety health inspectors make regular visits and also respond to accident reports or complaints about a plant, factory, or other workplace by interviewing workers or management—they may suspend activity that possibly poses a threat to workers. They write reports on safety standards that have been violated and describe conditions to be corrected. They may also discuss their findings with management to ensure standards will be promptly met.

Alcohol, tobacco, and firearms inspectors ensure compliance with laws governing taxes, competition, trade practices, and operating procedures. They inspect wineries, breweries, and distilleries; cigar and cigarette factories; explosives and firearms dealers, manufacturers, and users; and wholesale liquor dealers and importers. These inspectors work for the Treasury Department of the federal government, and their main concern is that all revenue on these various commodities be collected.

Requirements

There is such a variety of skills involved in these inspection jobs that the qualifications and education required depend on the area of work.

High School

The minimum education required to be a health or regulatory inspector is generally a bachelor's degree. In high school, therefore, you should take college preparatory classes. Concentrate on the sciences, such as courses in biology, chemistry, and health. Family and consumer science will also be useful to you. In addition, take courses in English and speech, because inspectors must communicate orally and in writing with the people whose facilities they are inspecting. Inspectors must also make reports to the agencies that employ them, so be sure to take computer classes that familiarize you with using this tool. Mathematics classes will also help round out your educational background. Finally, if your school offers any agricultural classes, be sure to take those. Agricultural classes will give you exposure to this field and allow you to test out your interest in working in this area.

Postsecondary Training

The specific degree and training qualifications vary for each position and area in which inspection is done. For federal positions, a civil service examination is generally required. Education and experience in the specific field is usually necessary.

A combination of classroom and on-the-job training in inspection procedure and applicable law is the usual preparation for inspection positions at the state and local as well as the federal level. College students should focus on general classes in speech, English (especially writing), business, computer science, and general mathematics. Those who have settled on a specific career in agriculture-related health and regulatory inspection may focus on classes in biology, health, chemistry, agriculture, and earth science or the environment.

Inspectors in the federal government must pass the Professional and Administrative Career Examination to work in such areas as consumer safety; alcohol, tobacco, and firearms; occupational safety and health; and customs and immigration. A bachelor's degree and three years' work experience are required to take this examination. Course work and other preparation must be related to the job. For example, applicants for food inspector positions must pass an examination based on specialized knowledge.

A bachelor's degree in the physical or biological sciences or in environmental health is required for sanitarians or environmental health inspectors.

Certification or Licensing

Certification and licensing requirements vary according to the position. The following is a sampling of these requirements.

As stated above, inspectors in the federal government must pass the Professional and Administrative Career Examination.

No written examination is required for agricultural commodity graders and quarantine inspectors, but they need experience and education in agricultural science.

A majority of states require licensing for sanitarians or environmental health inspectors. You will need to find out the requirements for the state in which you hope to work.

Other Requirements

Health and regulatory inspectors must be precision-minded, be able to make decisions, and be willing to accept responsibility. They must be tenacious and patient as they follow each case from investigation to its conclusion. They also must be able to communicate well with others in order to reach a clear analysis of a situation and be able to report this information to a superior or coworker. Inspectors must be able to write effective reports that convey vast amounts of information and investigative work. Depending on the inspector's area of work, an interest in agriculture, food processing, or even the environment will also make him or her a more dedicated employee. Finally, an inspector should be trustworthy as this is a position combining both power and the public trust.

Exploring

If you are interested in working as a health or regulatory inspector in the agricultural field, you may learn more by talking with people who are employed as inspectors. If you don't know anyone in this position, ask your high school guidance counselor to help you locate someone and set up an informational interview. Be prepared to ask questions when you get to the interview: What is an average day for this inspector like? What education and training background does he or she have? What is the best part of the job? If you show a genuine interest in the inspector's work, he or she will probably be glad to share insights with you.

Look for summer or part-time employment in a specific area that interests you, such as food preparation. Even a job at the local Dairy Queen will give you a basic knowledge of the legal requirements for food preparation and storage. You may also want to join your school's chapter of the National FFA Organization (formerly Future Farmers of America) as another way to explore aspects of this work. Through this club you may have the opportunity to work on agricultural projects involving plants or animals, which can give you a familiarity with regulations and procedures. The armed forces can provide you with valuable training and preparation in such areas as transportation.

Employers

The federal government employs the majority of inspectors in certain areas, such as food and agriculture, which come under the U.S. Public Health Service or the Department of Agriculture. Most environmental health inspectors work for state and local governments. Consumer safety is evenly divided between local government and the U.S. Food and Drug Administration.

Starting Out

Applicants may enter the occupations by applying to take the appropriate civil service examinations. Education in specific areas may be required. Some positions require a degree or other form of training. Others need considerable on-the-job experience in the field.

The civil service commissions for state and local employment will provide information on health and regulatory inspection positions under their jurisdiction. The federal government provides information on available jobs at local offices of the employment service, at the U.S. Office of Personnel Management, and at Federal Job Information Centers. The specific agency concerned with a job area can also be contacted.

Advancement

Advancement for health and regulatory inspectors in the federal government is based on the civil service promotion and salary structure. Advancement is automatic, usually at one-year intervals, for those people whose work is satisfactory. Additional education may also contribute to advancement to supervisory positions.

Advancements for health and regulatory inspectors in state and local government and in private industry are often similar to those offered at the federal level.

Earnings

According to the U.S. Department of Labor, most federally employed health and regulatory inspectors received average starting salaries around $25,500 to $31,200 in 1999. The median annual salary for all inspectors, except those in construction, is $36,820, and some earn more than $72,280.

Salaries vary greatly. Examples of annual average salaries (including nonsupervisory, supervisory, and management positions) paid by the federal government to experienced health and regulatory inspectors in 1999, according to the U.S. Department of Labor, include the following: safety and occupational health inspectors receive about $54,000; agricultural commodity graders, $41,600; food inspectors, $35,200; inspectors for consumer safety, $37,300; and quality assurance inspectors, $50,600.

Health and regulatory inspectors for state and local governments generally earn salaries lower than those paid by the federal government.

Health and regulatory inspectors also receive other benefits including paid vacation and sick days, health and dental insurance, pensions, and life insurance. Most inspectors enjoy the use of an official automobile and reimbursement for travel expenses.

Other health and regulatory inspectors receive additional benefits. Inspectors employed by the Food and Drug Administration (FDA) are eligible for bonuses based on their individual performance. These range from $100 to $5,000 or 10 percent of base pay, whichever is less.

Most federal inspectors, including employees of the FDA, are eligible to take advantage of the Federal Flexible Workplace (Flexiplace) Project, which permits employees to work at home or other approved sites for a portion of the workweek.

Work Environment

Most health and regulatory inspectors should expect to travel a considerable amount of the time. They will interact with a wide variety of people from different educational and professional backgrounds. Health and regulatory inspectors sometimes work long and irregular hours. Sometimes, inspectors will experience stressful, unpleasant, and even dangerous situations. Agricultural and food inspection may bring contact with unpleasant odors, loud noises, potentially infectious diseases, and other difficult working conditions. Agricultural commodity graders may work outside in the heat or in cool refrigeration units. They may also be required to lift heavy objects. Consumer safety inspectors may work in slaughterhouses or processing rooms or in refrigerated storage rooms. Environmental health inspectors may encounter radioactive or toxic materials or substances as they strive to make all areas of the environment safe for the average citizen.

Inspectors may face adversarial situations with individuals or organizations who feel that they do not warrant an investigation, are above the law, or are being singled out for inspection.

The work of health and regulatory inspectors is important and can be rewarding. Compensation and job security are generally good, and travel and automobile expenses are reimbursed when necessary. Inspectors can be proud that their skilled performance of their duties improves life in one way or another for every member of our society.

Outlook

Government workers are generally affected to a lesser degree by economic changes than are many other workers. The employment of health and regulatory inspectors is likely to grow about as fast as the average rate for all professions through 2008, according to the U.S. Department of Labor. This reflects growing public expectations and interest concerning the environment, safety concerns, and quality products. These interests, however, may be offset by the growing debate concerning oversized and ineffective government and the desire for fewer regulations and strictures on daily life.

Some employment growth will occur at local levels, especially in the regulation and compliance of water pollution and solid and hazardous waste disposal. Growth will also occur if more power and responsibilities are transferred to the states from the federal government. In private industry some job growth may occur as a result of increased enforcement of government regulations and company policy.

Most job opportunities will arise as a result of people retiring, transferring to other positions, or leaving the labor force for a variety of other reasons.

For More Information

To learn more about these agencies and for employment information, contact:

Occupational Safety and Health Administration
U.S. Department of Labor
Public Affairs Office, Room N3647
200 Constitution Avenue
Washington, DC 20210
Tel: 202-693-1999
Web: http://www.osha.gov

U.S. Department of Health and Human Services
200 Independence Avenue, SW
Washington, DC 20201
Tel: 877-696-6775
Web: http://www.hhs.gov

Canadian Public Health Association
1565 Carling Avenue, Suite 400
Ottawa, ON K1Z 8R1, Canada
Tel: 613-725-3769
Web: http://www.cpha.ca

Range Managers

School Subjects
Biology
Earth science

Personal Skills
Leadership/management
Technical/scientific

Work Environment
Indoors and outdoors
Primarily multiple locations

Minimum Education Level
Bachelor's degree

Salary Range
$20,600 to $31,200 to $46,300

Certification or Licensing
Voluntary

Outlook
About as fast as the average

Overview

Range managers work to maintain and improve grazing lands on public and private property. They research, develop, and carry out methods to improve and increase the production of forage plants, livestock, and wildlife without damaging the environment; develop and carry out plans for water facilities, erosion control, and soil treatments; restore rangelands that have been damaged by fire, pests, and undesirable plants; and manage the upkeep of range improvements, such as fences, corrals, and reservoirs.

History

Early in the history of the world, primitive peoples grazed their livestock wherever forage was plentiful. As the supply of grass and shrubs became depleted, they simply moved on, leaving the stripped land to suffer the effects of soil erosion. When civilization grew and the nomadic tribes began to establish settlements, people began to recognize the need for conservation and developed simple methods of land terracing, irrigation, and the rotation of grazing lands.

Much the same thing happened in the United States. The rapid expansion across the continent in the 19th century was accompanied by the destruction of plant and animal life and the abuse of the soil. Because the country's natural resources appeared inexhaustible, the cries of alarm that came from a few concerned conservationists went unheeded. It was not until after 1890 that conservation became a national policy. Today several state and federal agencies are actively involved in protecting the nation's soil, water, forests, and wildlife.

Rangelands cover more than a billion acres of the United States, mostly in the western states and Alaska. Many natural resources are found there: grass and shrubs for animal grazing, wildlife habitats, water from vast watersheds, recreation facilities, and valuable mineral and energy resources. In addition, rangelands are used by scientists who conduct studies of the environment.

The Job

Range managers are sometimes known as *range scientists*, *range ecologists*, or *range conservationists*. Their goal is to maximize range resources without damaging the environment. They accomplish this in a number of ways.

To help ranchers attain optimum livestock production, range managers study the rangelands to determine the number and kind of livestock that can be most profitably grazed, the grazing system to use, and the best seasons for grazing. The system they recommend must be designed to conserve the soil and vegetation for other uses, such as wildlife habitats, outdoor recreation, and timber.

Grazing lands must continually be restored and improved. Range managers study plants to determine which varieties are best suited to a particular range and to develop improved methods for reseeding. They devise biological, chemical, or mechanical ways of controlling undesirable and poisonous plants, and they design methods of protecting the range from grazing damage.

Range managers also develop and help carry out plans for water facilities, structures for erosion control, and soil treatments. They are responsible for the construction and maintenance of such improvements as fencing, corrals, and reservoirs for stock watering.

Although a great deal of range managers' time is spent outdoors, they also spend some time in offices, consulting with other conservation specialists, preparing written reports, and doing administrative work.

Rangelands have more than one use, so range managers often work in such closely related fields as wildlife and watershed management, forest management, and recreation. *Soil conservationists* and *naturalists* are concerned with maintaining ecological balance both on the range and in the forest preserves.

Requirements

High School

If you are interested in pursuing a career in range management, you should begin planning your education early. Since you will need a college degree for this work, take college preparatory classes in high school. Your class schedule should include the sciences, such as earth science, biology, and chemistry. Take mathematics and economics classes. Any courses that teach you to work with a computer will also be beneficial. You will frequently use this tool in your career to keep records, file reports, and do planning. English courses will also help you develop your research, writing, and reading skills. You will need all of these skills in college and beyond.

Postsecondary Training

The minimum educational requirement for range managers is usually a bachelor's degree in range management or range science. To be hired by the federal government, you will need at least 42 credit hours in plant, animal, or soil sciences and natural resources management courses, including at least 18 hours in range management. If you would like a teaching or research position, you will need a graduate degree in range management. Advanced degrees may also prove helpful for advancement in other jobs.

To receive a bachelor's degree in range management, students must have acquired a basic knowledge of biology, chemistry, physics, mathematics, and communication skills. Specialized courses in range management combine plant, animal, and soil sciences with the principles of ecology and resource management. Students are also encouraged to take electives, such as economics, forestry, hydrology, agronomy, wildlife, and computer science.

While a number of schools offer some courses related to range management, only about 35 colleges and universities have degree programs in range management or range science or in a discipline with a range management or range science option.

Certification or Licensing

The Society for Range Management offers certification as a Certified Range Management Consultant or a Certified Professional in Rangeland Management. These are voluntary certifications but demonstrate a professional's commitment to the field and the high quality of his or her work. Requirements include having a bachelor's degree and at least five years of experience in the field as well as passing a written exam.

Other Requirements

Along with their technical skills, range managers must be able to speak and write effectively and to work well with others. Range managers need to be self-motivated and flexible. They are generally persons who do not want the restrictions of an office setting and a rigid schedule. They should have a love for the outdoors as well as good health and physical stamina for the strenuous activity that this occupation requires.

Exploring

As a high school student, you can test your appetite for outdoor work by applying for summer jobs on ranches or farms. Other ways of exploring this occupation include a field trip to a ranch or interviews with or lectures by range managers, ranchers, or conservationists. Any volunteer work with conservation organizations—large or small—will give you an idea of what range managers do and will help you when you apply to colleges and for employment.

As a college student, you can get more direct experience by applying for summer jobs in range management with such federal agencies as the Forest Service, the Natural Resource Conservation Service, and the Bureau of Land

Management. This experience may better qualify you for jobs when you graduate.

Employers

The majority of range managers are employed by the federal government in the Bureau of Land Management or the Natural Resource Conservation Service. State governments employ range managers in game and fish departments, state land agencies, and extension services.

In private industry, the number of range managers is increasing. They work for coal and oil companies to help reclaim mined areas, for banks and real estate firms to help increase the revenue from landholdings, and for private consulting firms and large ranches. Some range managers with advanced degrees teach and do research at colleges and universities. Others work overseas with U.S. and U.N. agencies and with foreign governments.

Starting Out

The usual way to enter this occupation is to apply directly to the appropriate government agencies. People interested in working for the federal government may contact the Department of Agriculture's Forest Service or Natural Resource Conservation Service, or the Department of the Interior's Bureau of Indian Affairs or Bureau of Land Management. Others may apply to local state employment offices for jobs in state land agencies, game and fish departments, or agricultural extension services. Your college placement office should have listings of available jobs.

Advancement

Range managers may advance to administrative positions in which they plan and supervise the work of others and write reports. Others may go into teaching or research. It should be remembered that an advanced degree is often necessary for the higher-level jobs in this occupational field. Another way for range managers to advance is to enter business for themselves as range management consultants or ranchers.

Earnings

According to the U.S. Department of Labor, range managers with a bachelor's degree working for the federal government had starting salaries of between $20,600 and $25,500 in 1999. Those with master's degrees started at between $25,500 and $31,200, while those with doctorates started at $37,700 or more. Variations in salaries depended on such factors as academic achievement and location of the job. The average salary for range managers working for the federal government in nonsupervisory, supervisory, and managerial roles was $46,300 in 1999. State governments and private companies pay their range managers salaries that are about the same as those paid by the federal government. Range managers are also eligible for paid vacations and sick days, health and life insurance, and other benefits.

Work Environment

Range managers, particularly those just beginning their careers, spend a great deal of time on the range. That means they must work outdoors in all kinds of weather. They usually travel by car or small plane, but in rough country they use four-wheel-drive vehicles or get around on horseback or on foot. When riding the range, managers may spend a considerable amount of time away from home, and the work is often quite strenuous.

As range managers advance to administrative jobs, they spend more time working in offices, writing reports, and planning and supervising the work of others. Range managers may work alone or under direct supervision; often they work as part of a team. In any case, they must deal constantly with people—not only their superiors and co-workers but with the general public, ranchers, government officials, and other conservation specialists.

Outlook

This is a small occupation, and most of the openings will arise when older, experienced range managers retire or leave the occupation. The U.S. Department of Labor predicts that job growth will be about as fast as the average through 2008 for conservation scientists and foresters, a category that includes range managers. The need for range managers should be stimulated by a growing demand for wildlife habitats, recreation, and water as well as by an increasing concern for the environment. A greater number of large ranches will employ range managers to improve range management practices and increase output and profitability. Range specialists will also be employed in larger numbers by private industry to reclaim lands damaged by oil and coal exploration.

An additional demand for range managers could be created by the conversion of rangelands to other purposes, such as wildlife habitats and recreation. Federal employment for these activities, however, depends upon the passage of legislation concerning the management of range resources, an area that is always controversial. Smaller budgets may also limit employment growth in this area.

For More Information

Career and education information may be obtained from:

National Recreation and Park Association
22377 Belmont Ridge Road
Ashburn, VA 20148
Tel: 703-858-0784
Web: http://www.activeparks.com

This organization has career, education, scholarship, and certification information. Student membership is also available through its International Student Conclave.

Society for Range Management
445 Union Boulevard, Suite 230
Lakewood, CO 80228
Tel: 303-986-3309
Web: http://www.srm.org

For information about career opportunities in the federal government, contact:

U.S. Department of Agriculture
Natural Resources Conservation Service
14th and Independence Avenue
Washington, DC 20250
Web: http://www.nrcs.usda.gov

U.S. Department of Agriculture
U.S. Forest Service
PO Box 96090
Washington, DC 20090-6090
Web: http://www.fs.fed.us

U.S. Department of the Interior
Bureau of Indian Affairs
1849 C Street, NW, MS-4542-MIB
Washington, DC 20240
Tel: 202-208-3711
Web: http://www.doi.gov/bureau-indian-affairs.html

U.S. Department of the Interior
Bureau of Land Management
1849 C Street, NW, Room 406-LS
Washington, DC 20240
Tel: 202-452-5125
Web: http://www.blm.gov/nhp

U.S. Department of the Interior
National Park Service
1849 C Street, NW (3127)
Washington, DC 20240
Tel: 202-208-5391
Web: http://www.nature.nps.gov

Soil Conservationists and Technicians

School Subjects

Agriculture
Biology
Earth science

Personal Skills

Helping/teaching
Technical/scientific

Work Environment

Indoors and outdoors
Primarily multiple locations

Minimum Education Level

Bachelor's degree

Salary Range

$20,600 to $48,900 to $75,330

Certification or Licensing

Voluntary

Outlook

About as fast as the average

Overview

Soil conservationists develop conservation plans to help farmers and ranchers, developers, homeowners, and government officials best use their land while adhering to government conservation regulations. They suggest plans to conserve and reclaim soil, preserve or restore wetlands and other rare ecological areas, rotate crops for increased yields and soil conservation, reduce water pollution, and restore or increase wildlife populations. They assess the land users' needs, costs, maintenance requirements, and the life expectancy of various conservation practices. They plan design specifications using survey and field information, technical guides, and engineering field manuals. Soil conservationists also give talks to various organizations to educate land users and the public in general about how to conserve and restore soil and water resources. Many of their recommendations are based on information provided to them by *soil scientists*.

Soil conservation technicians work more directly with land users by putting the ideas and plans of the conservationist into action. In their work they use basic engineering and surveying tools, instruments, and techniques. They perform engineering surveys and design and implement conservation practices like terraces and grassed waterways. Soil conservation technicians monitor projects during and after construction, and periodically revisit the site to evaluate the practices and plans.

History

In 1908, President Theodore Roosevelt appointed a National Conservation Commission to oversee the proper conservation of the country's natural resources. As a result, many state and local conservation organizations were formed, and Americans began to take a serious interest in preserving their land's natural resources.

During World War I, farmers—who wished to capitalize on the shortage of wheat—planted many thousands of acres of wheat, mostly in middle western states. The crop was repeated year after year, until the soil was depleted. This depletion of the soil and the destruction of the natural cover of the land by too much cultivation led to the disastrous dust storms of the mid-1930s.

As a result of what happened to the Dust Bowl, Congress established the Natural Resource Conservation Service of the U.S. Department of Agriculture in 1935. Because more than 800 million tons of topsoil had already been blown away by the winds over the plains, the job of reclaiming the land through wise conservation practices was not an easy one. In addition to the large areas of the Middle West which had become desert land, there were other badly eroded lands throughout the country.

Fortunately, emergency planning came to the aid of the newly established conservation program. The Civilian Conservation Corps (CCC) was created to help alleviate unemployment during the Great Depression of the 1930s. The CCC established camps in rural areas and assigned people to aid in many different kinds of conservation. Soil conservationists directed those portions of the CCC program designed to halt the loss of topsoil by wind and water action.

Much progress has been made in the years since the Natural Resource Conservation Service was established. Wasted land has been reclaimed and further loss has been prevented. Land-grant colleges have initiated programs to help farmers understand the principles and procedures of soil conservation. The Cooperative Research, Education and Extension Service (within the

Department of Agriculture) provides workers who are skilled in soil conservation to work with these programs.

Throughout the United States today there are several thousand federally appointed soil conservation districts. A worker employed by the government works in a particular district to demonstrate soil conservation to farmers and agricultural businesses. There are usually one or more professional soil conservationists and one or more soil conservation technicians working in each district.

The Job

Soil conservationists and technicians with the federal Natural Resource Conservation Service help scientists and engineers obtain preliminary data used to establish and maintain soil and water conservation plans. They may also work closely with landowners and operators to establish and maintain sound conservation practices in land management and use.

Conservationists oversee soil conservation technicians who assist with preliminary engineering surveys; lay out contours, terraces, tile drainage systems, and irrigation systems; plant grasses and trees; collect soil samples and gather information from field notes; improve woodlands; assist in farm pond design and management; make maps from aerial photographs; and inspect specific areas to determine conservation needs.

Some conservationists and technicians work for the Bureau of Land Management which oversees hundreds of millions of acres of public domain. Workers in this federal agency help survey publicly owned areas, and pinpoint land features to determine the best use of public lands. They may be called upon to supervise a four- to six-person surveying team in carrying out the actual survey.

Soil conservation technicians in the Bureau of Reclamation serve as assistants to civil, construction, materials, or general engineers. Their job is to oversee certain phases of such projects as the construction of dams, and irrigation planning. The Bureau's ultimate goal is the control of water and soil resources for the benefit of farm, home, and city.

The following short paragraphs describe some positions typically held by entry-level soil conservationists and technicians.

Range technicians work closely with range conservationists helping to manage rangeland, most of which is in the western part of the United States. They determine the value of rangeland, its grazing capabilities, erosion hazards, and livestock potential.

Physical science technician aides gather data in the field, studying the physical characteristics of the soil, mapping land, and producing aerial survey maps for use by soil conservationists.

Engineering technician aides conduct field tests and oversee some phases of construction on dams and irrigation projects. They manage water resources and perform soil-conservation services. They also measure acreage, place property boundaries, and define drainage areas on maps.

Cartographic survey technician aides work with *cartographers* (map makers) to survey the public domain, setting boundaries, pinpointing land features, and determining the most beneficial public use.

The following short paragraphs describe some of the positions held by more experienced soil conservationists and technicians.

Cartographic technicians perform technical work in mapping or charting the earth or graphically representing geographical information.

Geodetic technicians perform nonprofessional work in the analysis, evaluation, processing, computation, and selection of geodetic survey data. (Geodesy is the science of determining the size and shape of the earth, the intensity and direction of the force of gravity, and the elevation of points on or near the earth's surface.)

Physical science technicians help professional scientists calibrate and operate measuring instruments; mix solutions; make routine chemical analyses; and set up and operate test apparatus.

Surveying technicians perform surveys for field measurement and mapping; to lay out construction; to check the accuracy of dredging operations; or to provide reference points and lines for related work. They gather data for the design and construction of highways, dams, topographic maps, and nautical or aeronautical charts.

Range conservationists administer and operate programs to properly conserve, develop, and utilize lands and related resources. They also serve to stabilize the livestock industry, which depends upon the range for its existence.

Requirements

High School

While in high school, you should take at least one year of algebra, enough English to be articulate and convincing in speech and writing, and one year of biology. If you are interested in areas of soil conservation involving direct contact with farmers and ranchers, high school courses in vocational agriculture are strongly recommended.

Postsecondary Training

Conservationists hold bachelor degrees in areas such as general agriculture, range management, crop or soil science, forestry, or agricultural engineering. Teaching and research positions require further graduate level education in a natural resources field. Though government jobs do not necessarily require a college degree (a combination of appropriate experience and education can serve as substitute), a college education can make you more desirable for a position.

Typical beginning courses include applied mathematics, communications skills, basic soils, botany, chemistry, zoology, and introduction to range management. Advanced courses include American government, surveying, forestry, game management, soil and water conservation, economics, fish management, and conservation engineering.

Conservationists and technicians must have some practical experience in the use of soil conservation techniques before they enter the field. Many schools require as part of their degree requirements work in the field during the school year or during summer vacation. Jobs are available in the federal park systems or with privately owned industries.

Certification or Licensing

No certification or license is required of soil conservationists and technicians; however, becoming certified could improve your skills and professional standing. The American Society of Agronomy offers certification in soil science.

Most government agencies require applicants to take a competitive examination for consideration.

Other Requirements

Soil conservationists and technicians must be able to apply practical as well as theoretical knowledge to their work. They need to have a working knowledge of soil and water characteristics; be skilled in management of woodlands, wildlife areas, and recreation areas; and have a knowledge of surveying instruments and practices, mapping, and the procedures used for interpreting aerial photographs.

Soil conservationists and technicians should also be able to write clear, concise reports to demonstrate and explain the results of their tests, studies, and recommendations. It goes without saying that a love for the outdoors and an appreciation for all natural resources are essential for success and personal fulfillment in this job.

Exploring

One of the best ways for you to become acquainted with soil conservation work and technology is through summer or part-time work on a farm or natural park. Other ways to explore this career include joining a local chapter of the 4-H Club or National FFA Organization (formerly Future Farmers of America). Science courses that include lab sections, and mathematics courses that focus on practical problem-solving will also help give you a feel for this kind of work.

Employers

Two-thirds of all conservation workers are empoyed by the government. At the federal level, most soil conservationists and technicians work for the Natural Resource Conservation Service, the Bureau of Land Management, and the Bureau of Reclamation. Others work for agencies at the state and county level. Soil conservationists and technicians also work for private agencies and firms such as banks and loan agencies, mining or steel companies, and public utilities companies. A small percentage of workers are self-employed consultants that advise private industry owners and government agencies.

Starting Out

Most students gain outside experience by working a summer job in their area of interest. You can get information on summer positions through your school's placement office. Often, contacts made on summer jobs lead to permanent employment after graduation. College career counselors and faculty members are often valuable sources of advice and information in finding employment.

Most soil conservationists and technicians find work with state, county, or federal agencies. Specific details of the hiring procedure for these jobs vary according to the level of government in which the applicant is seeking work. In general, however, students begin the application procedure during the fourth semester of their program and should expect some form of competitive examination as part of the process. College placement personnel can help students find out about the details of application procedures. Often representatives of government agencies visit college campuses to explain employment possibilities to students and sometimes to recruit for their agencies.

Advancement

Soil conservationists and technicians usually start out with a local conservational district to gain experience and expertise before advancing to the state, regional, or national level.

In many cases, conservationists and technicians may continue their education while working by taking evening courses at a local college or technical institute. Federal agencies that employ conservationists and technicians have a policy of "promotion from within." Because of this policy, there is a continuing opportunity for such workers to advance through the ranks. The degree of advancement that all conservationists and technicians can expect in their working careers is determined by their aptitudes, abilities, and of course their desire to advance.

Workers seeking a more dramatic change can transfer their skills to related jobs outside the conservation industry, such as farming or land appraisal.

Earnings

The majority of soil conservationists and technicians work for the federal government, and their salaries are determined by their government service rating. In 1999, the average annual salary for soil conservationists employed by the federal government was $48,900, according to the *Occupational Outlook Handbook*. Starting salaries ranged from $20,600 to $25,500 depending on academic achievement. Those with master's degrees could earn a higher starting salary ranging from $25,500 to $31,200, and with a doctorate, $37,700.

The salaries of conservationists and technicians working for private firms or agencies will be roughly comparable to those paid by the federal government. Earnings at the state and local levels vary depending on the region, but are typically lower.

Government jobs and larger private industries offer comprehensive benefit packages, usually more generous than those offered at smaller firms.

Work Environment

Soil conservationists and technicians usually work 40 hours per week, except in unusual or emergency situations. They have opportunities to travel, especially those employed by federal agencies.

Soil conservation is an outdoor job. Workers travel to work sites by car, but must often walk great distances to an assigned area. Although they sometimes work from aerial photographs and other on-site pictures, they cannot work from pictures alone. They must visit the spot that presents the problem in order to make appropriate recommendations.

Although soil conservationists and technicians spend much of their working time outdoors, office work is also necessary when generating detailed reports of their work to agency offices.

In their role as assistants to professionals, soil conservation technicians often assume the role of government public relations representatives when dealing with landowners and land managers. They must be able to explain the underlying principles of the structures that they design and the surveys that they perform.

To meet these and other requirements of the job, conservationists and technicians should be prepared to continue their education both formally and informally throughout their careers. They must stay aware of current periodicals and studies so that they can keep up-to-date in their area of specialization.

Soil conservationists and technicians gain satisfaction from knowing that their work is vitally important to the economy of the nation. Without their expertise, large portions of land in the United States could become barren within a generation.

Outlook

According to the U.S. Department of Labor, employment is expected to grow about as fast as the average in this field. Most soil conservationists and technicians are employed by the federal government; therefore, employment opportunities will depend in large part on levels of government spending. It is always difficult to predict future government policies; however, the need for government involvement in protecting natural resources will remain strong. The vast majority of America's cropland has suffered from some sort of erosion, and only continued efforts by soil conservation professionals can prevent a dangerous depletion of our most valuable resource: fertile soil.

Some soil conservationists and technicians are employed as research and testing experts for public utility companies, banks and loan agencies, and mining or steel companies. At present, a relatively small number of soil conservation workers are employed by these firms or agencies. However, decreased levels of employment by the federal government could lead to increased employment in these areas.

For More Information

For information on soil conservation careers and certification, contact:

American Society of Agronomy
Career Development and Placement Service
677 South Segoe Road
Madison, WI 53711
Tel: 608-273-8080
Email: headquarters@Agronomy.org
Web: http://www.agronomy.org

For more information on education and opportunities in the agricultural field, contact:

4-H
Stop 2225
1400 Independence Avenue, SW
Washington, DC 20250-2225
Tel: 202-720-2908
Web: http://www.4h-usa.org

National FFA Organization
6060 FFA Drive
PO Box 68960
Indianapolis, IN 46268
Tel: 317-802-6060
Web: http://www.ffa.org

For information on government soil conservation careers, contact:

Natural Resources Conservation Service
U.S. Department of Agriculture
Attn: Conservation Communications Staff
14th and Independence Avenues
Washington, DC 20250
Web: http://www.nrcs.usda.gov

For information on careers in soil conservation and certification, contact:

Soil and Water Conservation Society
7515 NE Ankeny Road
Ankeny, IA 50021
Tel: 515-289-2331
Web: http://www.swcs.org

Soil Scientists

School Subjects
Agriculture
Earth science

Personal Skills
Leadership/management
Technical/scientific

Work Environment
Indoors and outdoors
Primarily multiple locations

Minimum Education Level
Bachelor's degree

Salary Range
$24,200 to $53,600 to $80,000+

Certification or Licensing
Voluntary

Outlook
About as fast as the average

Overview

Soil scientists study the physical, chemical, and biological characteristics of soils to determine the most productive and effective planting strategies. Their research aids in producing larger, healthier crops and more environmentally sound farming procedures.

History

Two hundred years ago, farmers planted crops without restriction, unaware that soil could be depleted of necessary nutrients by overuse. When crops were poor, farmers often blamed the weather instead of their farming techniques. (Some parts of the world still blame supernatural forces for poor harvests.)

Soil—one of our most important natural resources—was taken for granted until its condition became too bad to ignore. An increasing population, moreover, made the United States aware that its own welfare depends on fertile soil capable of producing food for hundreds of millions of people.

Increasing concerns about feeding a growing nation brought agricultural practices into consideration and reevaluation. In 1862, the U.S. Department of Agriculture (USDA) was created to give farmers information about new crops and improved farming techniques. Although the department started small, today the USDA is one of the largest agencies of the federal government.

Following the creation of a seperate federal agency, laws were created to further promote and protect farmers. The 1933 Agricultural Adjustment Act inaugurated a policy of giving direct government aid to farmers. Two years later, the Natural Resource Conservation Service developed after disastrous dust storms blew away millions of tons of valuable topsoil and destroyed fertile cropland throughout the Midwestern states.

Since 1937, states have organized themselves into soil conservation districts. Each local division coordinates with the USDA, assigning soil scientists and soil conservationists to help local farmers establish and maintain farming practices that will use land in the wisest possible ways.

The Job

Soil is formed by the breaking of rocks and the decay of trees, plants, and animals. It may take as long as 500 years to make just one inch of topsoil. Unwise and wasteful farming methods can destroy that inch of soil in just a few short years. In addition, rainstorms may carry thousands of pounds of precious topsoil away and dissolve necessary chemicals to grow healthy crops through a process called erosion. Soil scientists work with engineers to address these issues.

Soil scientists spend much of their time outdoors, tramping over fields, advising farmers on crop rotation or fertilizers, assessing the amount of field drainage, and taking soil samples. After researching an area, they may suggest certain crops to farmers to protect bare earth from the ravages of the wind and weather.

Soil scientists may also specialize in one particular aspect of the work. For example, they may work as a *soil mapper* or *soil surveyor*. These specialists study soil structure, origin, and capabilities through field observations, laboratory examinations, and controlled experimentation. Their investigations are aimed at determining the most suitable uses for a particular soil.

Soil fertility experts develop practices that will increase or maintain crop size. They must consider both the type of soil and the crop planted in their analysis. Various soils react differently when exposed to fertilizers, soil additives, crop rotation, and other farming techniques.

All soil scientists work in the laboratory. They examine soil samples under the microscope to determine bacterial and plant-food components. They must also write reports based on their field notes and analysis done within the lab.

Soil science is part of the science of agronomy, which encompasses crop science. Soil and *crop scientists* work together in agricultural experiment stations during all seasons, doing research on crop production, soil fertility, and various kinds of soil management.

Some soil and crop scientists travel to remote sections of the world in search of plants and grasses that may thrive in this country and contribute to our food supply, pasture land, or soil replenishing efforts. Some scientists go overseas to advise farmers in other countries on how to treat their soils. Those with advanced degrees teach college agriculture courses and conduct research projects.

Requirements

High School

If you're interested in pursuing a career in agronomy, you should take college preparatory courses covering subjects such as math, science, English, and public speaking. Science and math classes will help you build a strong foundation for future intensive college courses. You should also take writing and speech courses because soil scientists must write and orally report their findings.

Postsecondary Training

A bachelor's degree in agriculture or soil science is the minimum educational requirement to become a soil scientist. Typical courses include physics, geology, bacteriology, botany, chemistry, soil and plant morphology, soil fertility, soil classification, and soil genesis.

Research and teaching positions usually require higher levels of education. Most colleges of agriculture also offer master's and doctoral degrees. In addition to studying agriculture or soil science, students can also specialize in biology, chemistry, physics, or engineering.

Certification or Licensing

Though not required, many soil scientists may seek certification to enhance their career. The American Society of Agronomy offers certification programs in the following areas: crop advisory, agronomy, crop science, soil science, plant pathology, and weed science. In order to be accepted into a program, applicants must meet certain levels of education and experience.

Other Requirements

Soil scientists must be able to work effectively alone and with others on projects, either outdoors or in the lab. Technology is used increasingly in this profession; an understanding of word processing, the Internet, multimedia software, databases, and even computer programming can be useful in the profession. Soil scientists spend many hours outdoors in all kinds of weather, so they must be able to endure sometimes difficult and uncomfortable physical conditions.

Exploring

If you live in an agricultural community, it may be easy to find opportunities for part-time or summer work on a farm or ranch. The National FFA Organization (formerly Future Farmers of America) can introduce you to the concerns of farmers and researchers. A 4-H club can also give you valuable experience in agriculture. Contact the local branch of these organizations, your county's soil conservation department, or other government agencies to learn about regional projects.

Employers

Most soil scientists work for state or federal departments of agriculture. However, they may also work for less obvious public employers, such as land appraisal boards, land-grant colleges and universities, and conservation departments. Soil scientists who work overseas may be employed by the U.S. Agency for International Development.

Soil scientists are needed in private industries as well, such as agricultural service companies, banks, insurance and real estate firms, food products companies, wholesale distributors, and environmental and engineering consulting groups. Private firms may hire soil scientists for sales or research positions.

Starting Out

In the public sector, college graduates can apply directly to the Resources Conservation Service of the Department of Agriculture, the Department of the Interior, the Environmental Protection Agency, or other state government agencies for beginning positions. University placement services generally have listings for these openings as well as opportunities available in private industry.

Advancement

Salary increases are the most common form of advancement for soil scientists. The nature of the job may not change appreciably even after many years of service. Higher administrative and supervisory positions are few in comparison with the number of jobs that must be done in the field.

Opportunities for advancement will be higher for those with advanced degrees. For soil scientists engaged in teaching, advancement may translate into a higher academic rank with more responsibility. In private business firms, soil scientists have opportunities to advance into positions such as department head or research director. Supervisory and manager positions are also available in state agencies such as road or conservation departments.

Earnings

According to the U.S. Department of Labor, median earnings in 1999 for agricultural scientists were $42,340. The lowest 10 percent earned less than $24,200; the middle 50 percent earned between $32,370 and $59,240; and the highest 10 percent, $79,820.

Federal salaries for soil scientists were higher; in 1999, they made an average of $53,600 a year. Government earnings greatly depend on levels of experience and education. Those with doctorates and a great deal of experience may be qualified for higher government positions, with salaries ranging from $67,000 to $87,000. Other than short-term research projects, most jobs offer health and retirement benefits in addition to your annual salary.

Work Environment

Most soil scientists work 40 hours a week. Their job is varied, ranging from field work collecting samples, to lab work analyzing their findings. Some jobs may involve travel—even to foreign countries. Other positions may include teaching or supervisory responsibilities for field training programs.

Outlook

The *Occupational Outlook Handbook* reports that employment within the field of soil science is expected to grow as fast as the average. The career of soil scientist will be affected by the government's involvement in farming studies; federal and state budget cuts will limit funding for this type of job. However, private businesses will continue to demand soil scientists for research and sales positions. Companies dealing with seed, fertilizers, or farm equipment are examples of private industries that hire soil scientists.

Technological advances in equipment and methods of conservation will allow scientists to better protect the environment, as well as improve farm production. Scientists' ability to evaluate soils and plants will improve with more precise research methods. Combine-mounted yield monitors will produce data as the farmer crosses the field, and satellites will provide more detailed field information. With computer images, scientists will also be able to examine plant roots more carefully.

A continued challenge facing future soil scientists will be convincing farmers to change their current methods of tilling and chemical treatment in favor of environmentally safer methods. They must encourage farmers to balance increased agricultural output with the protection of our limited natural resources.

For More Information

For information on career placement and certification, contact:

American Society of Agronomy
677 South Segoe Road
Madison, WI 53711
Tel: 608-273-8080
Web: http://www.agronomy.org

For more information on education and opportunities in the agricultural field, contact:

National FFA Organization
6060 FFA Drive
PO Box 68960
Indianapolis, IN 46268
Tel: 317-802-6060
Web: http://www.ffa.org

For information about membership, seminars, and issues affecting soil scientists, visit the NSCSS Web site.

National Society of Consulting Soil Scientists (NSCSS)
325 Pennsylvania Avenue, SE, Suite 700
Washington DC 20003
Tel: 800-535-7148
Web: http://www.nscss.org

For a career resources booklet, contact:

Soil Science Society of America
677 South Segoe Road
Madison, WI 53711
Tel: 608-273-8095
Web: http://www.soils.org